TEACHING LITERACY IN SECOND GRADE

TOOLS FOR TEACHING LITERACY

Donna Ogle and Camille Blachowicz, Series Editors

This highly practical series includes two kinds of books: (1) grade-specific titles for first-time teachers or those teaching a particular grade for the first time; (2) books on key literacy topics that cut across all grades, such as integrated instruction, English language learning, and comprehension. Written by outstanding educators who know what works based on extensive classroom experience, each research-based volume features hands-on activities, reproducibles, and best practices for promoting student achievement.

TEACHING LITERACY IN SIXTH GRADE
Karen Wood and Maryann Mraz

TEACHING LITERACY IN KINDERGARTEN
Lea M. McGee and Lesley Mandel Morrow

INTEGRATING INSTRUCTION: LITERACY AND SCIENCE
Judy McKee and Donna Ogle

TEACHING LITERACY IN SECOND GRADE
Jeanne R. Paratore and Rachel L. McCormack

TEACHING LITERACY IN FIRST GRADE
Diane Lapp, James Flood, Kelly Moore, and Maria Nichols

TEACHING LITERACY
in Second Grade

Jeanne R. Paratore
Rachel L. McCormack

Series Editors' Note by Donna Ogle and Camille Blachowicz

THE GUILFORD PRESS
New York   London

© 2005 The Guilford Press
A Division of Guilford Publications, Inc.
72 Spring Street, New York, NY 10012
www.guilford.com

All rights reserved

Except as indicated, no part of this book may be reproduced, translated,
stored in a retrieval system, or transmitted, in any form or by any means,
electronic, mechanical, photocopying, microfilming, recording, or otherwise,
without written permission from the Publisher.

Printed in the United States of America

This book is printed on acid-free paper.

Last digit is print number: 9   8   7   6   5   4   3   2   1

LIMITED PHOTOCOPY LICENSE

These materials are intended for use only by qualified professionals.

The Publisher grants to individual purchasers of this book nonassignable
permission to reproduce all materials for which photocopying permission
is specifically granted in a footnote. This license is limited to you, the
individual purchaser, for use with your own clients or students. It does not
extend to additional professionals in your institution, school district, or
other setting, nor does purchase by an institution constitute a site license.
This license does not grant the right to reproduce these materials for
resale, redistribution, or any other purposes (including but not limited to
books, pamphlets, articles, video- or audiotapes, and handouts or slides for
lectures or workshops). Permission to reproduce these materials for these
and any other purposes must be obtained in writing from the Permissions
Department of Guilford Publications.

Library of Congress Cataloging-in-Publication Data

Paratore, Jeanne R.
  Teaching literacy in second grade / Jeanne R. Paratore and Rachel L.
McCormack.
      p.   cm. — (Tools for teaching literacy)
  Includes bibiographical references and index.
    ISBN 1-59385-177-4 (pbk.) — ISBN 1-59385-178-2 (hardcover)
    1. Language arts (Elementary).   2. Elementary school teaching.   3. Second
grade (Education).   I. McCormack, Rachel L.   II. Title.   III. Series.
  LB1573.P217   2005
  372.6—dc22

                                                                    2005004647

ABOUT THE AUTHORS

Jeanne R. Paratore, EdD, is Associate Professor of Education at Boston University, where she teaches courses in literacy, language, and cultural studies. From 1989 to 1997 she was an integral member of the Boston University/Chelsea, Massachusetts, Public School Partnership, a comprehensive urban school reform effort, in which she focused her efforts on improving classroom literacy instruction and building strong home–school partnerships. She was a core advisor to Teaching Reading, K–2, A Video Library of Effective Classroom Practices, a project funded by the Annenberg Foundation and produced by WGBH television. At present, Dr. Paratore works with school-based literacy leaders in Lowell, Massachusetts, to support effective instruction in classrooms throughout the city. She has written articles and book chapters about family literacy, classroom grouping practices, and classroom assessment.

Rachel L. McCormack, EdD, is Assistant Professor of Education at Roger Williams University, Bristol, Rhode Island, where she teaches courses in literacy education and children's literature. As a classroom teacher, she taught first, second, and fifth grades, and she served as a school-based reading specialist. Her research interests include classroom discourse and the effects of peer-led discussion on children's comprehension and learning, and the effects of professional development on schoolwide change in literacy instruction.

SERIES EDITORS' NOTE

As teacher educators and staff developers, we have become aware of the need for a series of books for thoughtful practitioners who want a practical, research-based introduction to teaching literacy at specific grade levels. Preservice and beginning teachers want to know how to be as effective as possible; they also know there are great differences in what students need across grade levels. We have met teacher after teacher who, when starting to teach or teaching a new grade, asked for a guide targeted at their specific grade level. Until now we have not had a resource to share with them.

We also collaborate with staff developers and study group directors who want effective inservice materials that they can use with teachers at many different levels yet that still provide specific insights for individual grade levels. Thus the Tools for Teaching Literacy series was created.

This series is distinguished by two innovative characteristics designed to make it useful to individual teachers, staff developers, and study groups alike. Each Tools for Teaching Literacy volume:

➤ Is written by outstanding educators who are noted for their knowledge of research, theory, and best practices; who spend time in real classrooms working with teachers; and who are experienced staff developers who work alongside teachers applying these insights in classrooms. We think the series authors are unparalleled in these qualifications.

➤ Is organized according to a structure shared by all the grade-level books, which include chapters on:

- the nature of the learner at a particular grade level
- appropriate goals for literacy

- setting up the physical environment for literacy
- getting to know students with appropriate assessments and planning for differentiation
- a week in the grade-level classroom—what this looks like in practice with important instructional strategies and routines
- resources for learning

With this common organization in the grade-level books, a staff developer can use several different volumes in the series for teacher study groups, new teacher seminars, and other induction activities, choosing particular discussion and learning topics, such as classroom organization, that cross grade-level concerns. Teachers can also easily access information on topics of most importance to them and make comparisons across the grade levels.

A second-grade classroom is an exciting place to visit. Children are consolidating their growing reading and writing expertise, exploring new genres, and becoming more effective communicators. In this volume, Jeanne R. Paratore and Rachel L. McCormack provide a road map of what teachers can do to optimize literacy learning for their students. The stops along the way in several teachers' classrooms provide clear images of what excellent instruction looks like in action.

DONNA OGLE
CAMILLE BLACHOWICZ

ACKNOWLEDGMENTS

We could not have written this book without the help of the four second-grade teachers who allowed us the privilege of visiting their classrooms many times, took countless phone calls to help us understand and clarify their beliefs and practices, shared with us copies of the lessons and materials they prepared, and gathered samples of children's work that demonstrated their instructional routines and practices. We are truly grateful to them for all of the ways they helped us, and we credit them (and the principals who allowed us into the classrooms) with deepening our understanding of how excellent teachers use evidence about effective practice to make a difference in children's literacy learning lives.

We are also grateful to the children in these classrooms, who so willingly went about their daily routines in the face of our intrusions and did their best to ignore our unsophisticated attempts to capture those routines on film; and although each child is special to us, Will, in particular, allowed us to reveal a good many details about his literacy behaviors and habits. His openness enabled us to begin our work with a truly genuine portrait. Connected to Will and our ability to tell Will's story are, of course, his mom and dad. In this case, his mom, Barbara, served as our "informant," and her detailed descriptions helped us to see, with increased clarity, that understanding children's literacy development requires knowledge about literacy practices at home, as well as at school.

Finally, we are grateful to Donna Ogle and Camille Blachowicz, whose vision for this series, generosity in including us, and thoughtful responses to our manuscript helped make us better teachers and better writers.

CONTENTS

CHAPTER 1
WHAT IS THE SECOND-GRADE CHILD LIKE?

In a visit to Vickie Kagan's second-grade classroom, we discovered the writing of a child named Will displayed on a wall in the writing center (Figure 1.1):

The Sloth and the Monkey

Once upon a time there was a sloth and a monkey. They were good friends with each other. Then the next day the Sloth got captured by the hunters. Then the Monkey tried to help his friend the Sloth by cutting the rope with a sharp rock.

Moral: Good friends help each other.

In another writing piece, this time as a statement of resolutions for the new year, Will wrote (Figure 1.2):

Eat more food.

Focus on the teacher.

Make mom & dad proud.

Be nice to my sister.

Make new friends.

In many ways, Will is typical of most second graders. Even in just two samples, we get some sense of what interests him as a 7-year-old. In fact, themes that child development theorists identify as central to children Will's age are evident in his writing: He cares deeply about his family, and even though he fusses a bit with his older sister, he wants to be nice to her. He, like other second graders, wants

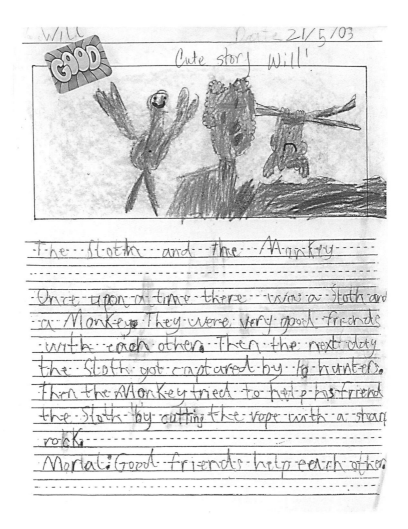

FIGURE 1.1. Will's writing.

very much to please his teacher. But, perhaps a bit unlike the average second grader, paying attention in school is not an easy task for Will. He has been identified as a child with attention deficit disorder, and he knows that staying focused requires a bit of extra effort. His mom and dad and his teacher know this too, and together they have figured out a plan that they think is working, at least on most days.

Like most second graders, Will loves to be read to, and he has wide reading interests. He told us he especially likes books that have elements of magic and

Will.

those that have central characters who are his age or a little bit older; and he said that he especially likes a story in which the characters fight evil or powerful enemies. In particular, he loves J. K. Rowling's Harry Potter books; his favorite among them is *Harry Potter and the Goblet of Fire*. He also loves *Midnight for Charlie Bone* by Jenny Nimmo, *Secret of Platform 13* by Eva Ibbotson, *Seven Day Magic* by Edward Eager, and *Artemis Fowl* by Eoin Colfer. His reading interests extend beyond his love of stories to include Rebecca Stefoff's nature books, and he has enjoyed *Ant*, *Jellyfish*, *Crab*, and *Chameleon*.

Despite his interest in reading, though, and his ability to comprehend sophisticated language and plot structures, Will struggles a bit to keep up with his peers. His teacher describes his performance as just a bit below what she considers to be the major benchmarks for second-grade readers. Although he is included in all grade-level reading tasks and texts, he receives substantial help from his teacher to be successful. He also has many opportunities in small-group meetings to read text that is matched to his instructional level. At home, Will and his mom and dad spend a lot of time with books, but most of the time, Will prefers that his parents read to him. His mom reports that this preference is slowly changing, but that it takes a lot of encouragement to get Will to read a complete picture book; he typically needs to be coaxed into doing the reading himself. She does this by promising to read to him after he reads, or by alternating pages with him—although he is, his mom said, "a manipulator." She explained that when they are sharing the reading responsibility, he will often claim that his page "has more words" than hers and argue that they need to trade turns. She said he likes choral reading, but she also noted that she is hesitant to do this because, she said with a chuckle, "he cheats." When he does read himself, he likes the series of *Miss Nelson* books by Harry Allard and almost any book by Robert Munsch.

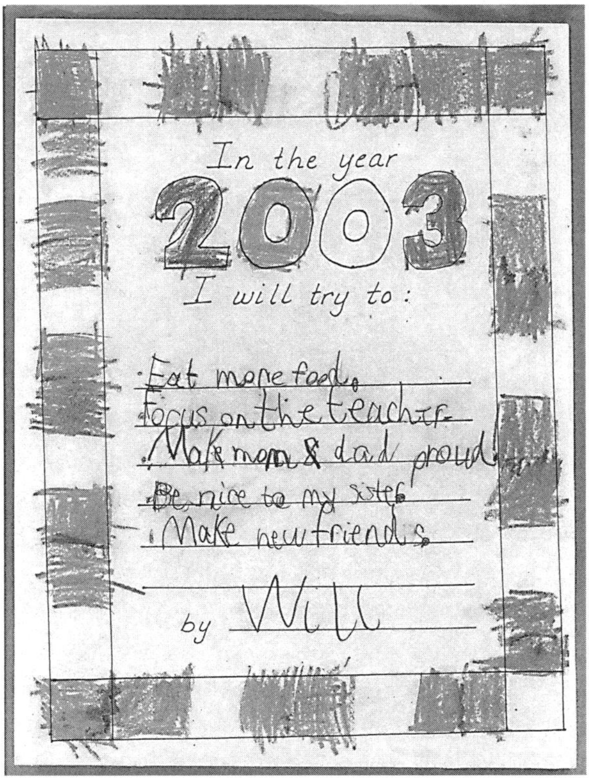

FIGURE 1.2. Will's New Year's resolutions.

There is much in Will's profile that represents the "typical" second-grade student. As we noted earlier, his reading and writing interests are a mirror image of what Huck, Heckler, Hickman, and Kiefer (2003) identify as themes and topics appropriate for 7- to 9-year-olds. They recommend, for example, books about the warmth and security of family relationships. They explain that books about families that resemble children's own can provide emotional comfort, whereas books about families different from their own can provide vicarious experiences that help them to develop understanding and empathy toward those who are different from them. Huck et al. also use developmental theory to predict that children in this age group may be working out the differences between reality and fantasy, and they suggest that fanciful books can support this development. They note that at this stage of development, many children especially enjoy stories in which a major element is magic—also an obvious favorite of Will's. They say that children within this age range are also developing their sense of humor; this developmental milestone, of course, fits with Will's love of the *Miss Nelson* books and those by Robert Munsch. The researchers also note that children of second-grade age show a strong and growing sense of justice, and they demand the application of rules, regardless of circumstances. This behavior, too, is consistent with Will's interests in books that portray characters in their fight against evil. In addition, Will is beginning to show interest in nonfiction texts, and this, too, is consistent with the reading behaviors of many second graders (Barone, 2003/2004). If Will is representative of second graders (and we think he is), then our experience with him suggests that if second-grade teachers use child development theory to guide their selection of books for instructional and recreational reading, they are likely to make good choices for most if not all of their students.

There are also details in Will's profile that likely are not representative of the typical second-grade student. For example, observations and evidence tell us that most second graders are on their way to at least the initial stages of reading independence; they take pride in their ability to read on their own and often want to "show off" their growing ability by reading aloud to teachers, peers, and family members. Will, as we have seen, often needs to be coaxed into independent reading.

In their study of the characteristics and behaviors of exemplary elementary teachers, Block, Oakar, and Hurt (2002) reported that one of the traits that differentiated excellent second-grade teachers was their ability to respond creatively to the range of needs that arises in the children in their classrooms. They explained that second-grade teachers were more likely than their earlier-grade colleagues to use one-on-one conferences "to relate to students in a personalized manner and provide the extra time second graders need to ask questions and receive targeted instruction to fill specific literacy gaps" (p. 190). Will's profile makes deeply apparent the need for excellent teachers to probe and uncover individual needs, interests, and talents. It reminds us that although evidence of what is typical can point us in the right direction, no two children are alike. Truly optimizing instruction so that we "leave no child behind" requires that we know what to expect of the children in our classrooms, but also that we know how to find out what makes every child special. In the pages that follow, we hope to help you do just that. Throughout each chapter, we base our suggestions on what we believe to be a simple but important premise: that good teachers (1) know *what* to teach; (2) know how to discover what students *already know* about reading and writing so that they can discern *when* to teach particular skills and strategies, and (3) know *how* to teach— that is, they know which instructional practices are most successful in *helping children learn*.

LOOKING BACKWARD AND FORWARD

We began our exploration of teaching reading and writing in second grade with an introduction to Will, a child we believe second-grade teachers will find quite familiar. By looking through the lens of Will's reading interests and motivations and his literacy and learning strengths and needs, we hoped to capture an image of what the second-grade child is like. At the same time, however, we do not mean to suggest that any one child is truly representative, for what makes teaching such an exciting (and challenging) enterprise is the recognition that each year, with each new "collection" of youngsters, we meet children unlike those we have met before.

We explained that, in our view, teachers who succeed at meeting this challenge possess three fundamental types of knowledge. They know what to teach: They have a reliable and validated source of both long- and short-range goals and benchmarks that represent what their students should know upon completion of their second-grade year; they also know which specific skills and strategies will help their students achieve identified goals and benchmarks. Next, they know when to teach: They have a system for determining what children know upon entry to their classrooms and a way to monitor their learning over time. They engage in classroom-based, curriculum-embedded assessment to determine what students already know so that they can determine the starting point for reaching or exceeding the stated goals. Finally, they know how to teach. That is, they are knowledgeable about instructional practices that consistently predict high levels of reading achievement, and they plan and implement daily and weekly instructional routines that are aligned with trustworthy evidence.

In the chapters that follow, we explore each of these three fundamental ideas in depth. In Chapter 2, we introduce two sources of knowledge about second-grade goals and benchmarks: *Standards for the English Language Arts* (International Reading Association and National Council of Teachers of English, 1996) and *Primary Literacy Standards* (New Standards Primary Literacy Committee, 1999). Our purpose is to answer two questions: (1) What evidence supports the importance of each identified area of knowledge for which children are expected to be held accountable?; and (2) What are the instructional implications?

In Chapter 3 we turn to the evidence related to the characteristics of classroom environments in which children excel in learning to read and write. We describe what we know and how typical second-grade teachers use the evidence to prepare their classroom learning environments and to develop classroom literacy routines. Then we visit a focal classroom where we observe the ways in which Pat Arterberry, a veteran second-grade teacher in New Bedford, Massachusetts, optimizes children's opportunities to learn and use literacy during the school day through thoughtful and purposeful arrangement of the classroom environment.

In Chapter 4 we focus on the ways expert teachers determine when to teach particular skills and strategies. We explore the ways effective teachers use classroom observations, interviews, running records, story retellings, written and oral summaries, and children's self-assessments to construct a profile of children's literacy strengths and needs. This time we travel to Nantucket, Massachusetts, where we talk with a relatively new teacher, Shauna DiLuca. She describes the ways in which she uses daily instructional events to inform her understanding of what children know and need to learn.

In Chapter 5 we examine the complex issue of how excellent teachers respond to the individual differences they uncover through good assessment. We address the challenge of differentiating instruction in two ways: by providing (1) strategies for grouping students in ways that optimize their opportunities to learn, and (2) strategies that help struggling readers access difficult texts. As in the earlier chapters, we begin by examining the research evidence that supports particular practices, and then we visit Karen Murray, who also teaches in Nantucket, Massachusetts, to observe the ways in which she uses research to organize her students and their literacy learning activities.

In Chapter 6 we integrate the ideas related to each of the fundamental principles—knowing what to teach, how to teach, and when to teach—as we "walk through" a typical week in the classroom of Vickie Kagan, in Anytown, Massachusetts.[1] Here you will have a chance to see how a veteran teacher joins her knowledge and understanding of effective instructional practices with her knowledge of the youngsters in her classroom. The week's activities are described using Vickie's own words, her written plans, photographs of classroom events and activities, and students' work samples.

In Chapter 7 we move beyond the confines of the classroom setting and explore the role that parents play in their children's academic success. The ideas presented in this chapter are based on two essential claims: First, when children receive parental support in learning to read and write, they have higher levels of academic achievement. Second, teachers can make a difference in the extent to which parents become involved in their children's learning. In presenting these ideas, rather than focus on specific classrooms, as in previous chapters, we have chosen to highlight particular practices that easily can be shaped for use in a multitude of settings. We describe three initiatives: (1) a monthly publication of a classroom newsletter, (2) the development of home literacy portfolios, and (3) a classroom storybook reading project. In each case we describe contexts in which parents, teachers, and children exchange information about a particular topic or practice, and then use that information to bridge uses of literacy practices at home and school.

Finally, in Chapter 8 we consider the resources that support teachers as they work to meet the learning standards intended to teach every child to read.

In the next stage of our journey, we set off to deepen our understanding of how excellent teachers respond to both the expected and unexpected needs of second-grade youngsters.

Try It Out

■ Think about the children in your second-grade classroom. What are their reading interests and how do they match the interests identified by child psychology theorists? Make a list of the similar interests you notice among the children in your classroom as well as a list of child-specific interests. Consider the ways you might use students' common interests to guide your selection of topics for class discussion and for reading. In addition, think about the ways you might use children's particular interests in addressing their special needs.

CHAPTER 2

KNOWING WHAT TO TEACH IN SECOND GRADE

In Chapter 1 we presented a portrait of Will, a child we consider to be like the children many second-grade teachers greet each morning. In this chapter we begin our examination of what second-grade youngsters such as Will need to know to achieve the benchmarks expected of them when they leave second grade. Our purpose is to answer two questions: (1) What evidence supports the importance of each identified area of knowledge? (2) What are the instructional implications?

In the first part of this chapter we present two groups of standards or benchmarks that leading professional literacy organizations have established to guide literacy instruction. After that, we explore what these standards actually mean for instruction—what are the essential instructional elements that children must acquire in order to meet the standards? To answer that question, we describe seven important areas of literacy research and theory: phonemic awareness, phonics, vocabulary, fluency, comprehension, writing, and motivation and interest. Each of these areas relates to one or more of the Standards for the English Language Arts (International Reading Association and National Council of Teachers of English, 1996) and the Primary Literacy Standards (New Standards Primary Literacy Committee, 1999). In each case, we provide a brief summary of related research and theory and a few brief examples of research-based teaching strategies. The remaining chapters provide more detailed examples of how the various instructional practices are implemented in the classrooms of "real" second-grade teachers.

WHAT WE EXPECT SECOND GRADERS TO KNOW AND DO

We begin this section with a cautionary statement: As we review what experts identify as common standards, we ask you to keep in mind that sameness is atypical in today's classrooms. What now makes a classroom "typical" is not the degree of similarity among children but the degrees of difference. Typical classrooms are those that represent children from many different language groups and cultures, children with a range of learning abilities and disabilities, children differently motivated and of varying interests. The skillful teacher is one who knows and recognizes the benchmarks that he or she should hold standard for every child, but also knows how to find strength in the children's diversity—how to build a common community while celebrating and nurturing the children's differences. The excellent classroom is one in which children such as Will—the second grader we met in Chapter 1—can find themselves in the books and the conversations that are shared by all, but can also find help in the special practices and techniques teachers use to accommodate their differences.

THE STANDARDS: KNOWING WHAT TO TEACH

Learning to read is a complex process in which individual needs are influenced by an array of cognitive, linguistic, and affective factors. As such, understanding and defining learning needs require information that extends far beyond children's age and grade placement. As a starting point in our exploration of what second-grade children need to know about reading and writing, we begin with the Standards for English the Language Arts, as defined by the International Reading Association (IRA) and the National Council of Teachers of English (NCTE, 1996; Figure 2.1). These standards are deliberately broad in nature, intended as a general framework for teaching reading and writing across grade levels and in diverse settings. Although such broad generalizations may, at first glance, seem unhelpful to the second-grade teacher, they are useful—indeed, even critically important—in underscoring the developmental nature of literacy learning and the importance of establishing, from the earliest stages, fundamental understandings about the nature of print and its place in our daily lives. As you read and review the standards, it is important to note that in introducing them, the IRA and the NCTE emphasized that, although the standards are presented as a list, "they are, in fact, interrelated and should be considered as a whole" (www.reading.org/advocacy/elastandards/standards.html, p. 1).

    After reading these standards you may be thinking that establishing long-term

1. Students read a wide range of print and nonprint texts to build an understanding of texts, of themselves, and of the cultures of the United States and the world; to acquire new information; to respond to the needs and demands of society and the workplace; and for personal fulfillment. Among these texts are fiction and nonfiction, classic and contemporary works.

2. Students read a wide range of literature from many periods in many genres to build an understanding of the many dimensions (e.g., philosophical, ethical, aesthetic) of human experience.

3. Students apply a wide range of strategies to comprehend, interpret, evaluate, and appreciate texts. They draw on their prior experiences, their interactions with other readers and writers, their knowledge of word meaning and of other texts, their word identification strategies, and their understanding of textual features (e.g., sound–letter correspondence, sentence structure, context, graphics).

4. Students adjust their use of spoken, written, and visual language (e.g., conventions, style, vocabulary) to communicate effectively with a variety of audiences and for different purposes.

5. Students employ a wide range of strategies as they write and use different writing process elements appropriately to communicate with different audiences for a variety of purposes.

6. Students apply knowledge of language structure, language conventions (e.g., spelling and punctuation), media techniques, figurative language, and genre to create, critique, and discuss print and nonprint texts.

7. Students conduct research on issues and interests by generating ideas and questions, and by posing problems. They gather, evaluate, and synthesize data from a variety of sources (e.g., print and nonprint texts, artifacts, people) to communicate their discoveries in ways that suit their purpose and audience.

8. Students use a variety of technological and information resources (e.g., libraries, databases, computer networks, video) to gather and synthesize information and to create and communicate knowledge.

9. Students develop an understanding of and respect for diversity in language use, patterns, and dialects across cultures, ethnic groups, geographic regions, and social roles.

10. Students whose first language is not English make use of their first language to develop competency in the English language arts and to develop understanding of content across the curriculum.

11. Students participate as knowledgeable, reflective, creative, and critical members of a variety of literacy communities.

12. Students use spoken, written, and visual language to accomplish their own purposes (e.g., for learning, enjoyment, persuasion, and the exchange of information).

FIGURE 2.1. Standards for the English language arts.

From International Reading Association: List of Standards from IRA and NCTE. (1996). *Standards for the English Language Arts.* Newark, DE: International Reading Association; and Urbana, IL: National Council of Teachers of English. Reprinted with permission of the International Reading Association.

goals is important, but that doing so may not necessarily help you to decide what to teach on any particular day. What day-to-day experiences and skills do children need to have if they are to realize these important goals? To help determine an answer to this question, we turn to the Primary Literacy Standards (New Standards Primary Literacy Committee, 1999). In Figure 2.2 we present a glimpse of the benchmarks detailed in these standards. (See Appendix A for the complete list of New Standards for second grade.) As you read them, notice the specificity and clarity of the benchmarks that accompany each standard. With these standards as a guide, a second-grade teacher could discern the particular achievements expected within important literacy domains: phonemic awareness, phonics, fluency, vocabulary, comprehension, writing, and motivation and interest. In the next section, we examine the evidence that validates the importance of helping each child achieve these benchmarks, and we begin to explore what we know about *how* to teach.

ELEMENTS THAT CONTRIBUTE TO STUDENTS' SUCCESS AT MEETING THE STANDARDS

Phonemic Awareness

Phonemic awareness is the ability to hear separate sounds in words and to manipulate those sounds. For example, a child who has phonemic awareness knows that the word *cat* has three sounds—/c/ /a/ /t/—and that the word *shop* also has three sounds—/sh/ /o/ /p/. Phonemic awareness is important because evidence indicates that it is foundational for success in learning to read (Snow, Burns, & Griffin, 1998). Children use their awareness and understanding of the sounds in words and of how sounds in words are segmented and blended to help them identify written words. They also use phonemic awareness to help them spell words. Many children acquire phonemic awareness before they come to school from the types of activities that are common to many family, community, and preschool contexts, such as being read to and reciting nursery rhymes, chants, and songs. But this is not the case for every child, and it may be difficult to pinpoint the precise reason for the absence of phonemic awareness skills. Some children have fewer opportunities to hear and play with language; others may have chronic ear infections or other hearing-related difficulties in early childhood that diminish their awareness of sounds in language.

Researchers have found very high rates of success when teachers provide students with explicit instruction in phonemic awareness (National Reading Panel Report, 2000). By the time children enter second grade, most who have had the benefit of excellent first-grade instruction have already acquired phonemic aware-

Reading Standard 1: Print–Sound Code

By the end of second grade, students should have a firm grasp of the print–sound code and be able to read the full range of English spelling patterns. By the end of the year, we expect second-grade students to:

- read regularly spelled one- and two-syllable words automatically; and
- recognize or figure out most irregularly spelled words and such spelling patterns as diphthongs, special vowel spellings and common word endings.

Reading Standard 2: Getting the Meaning

Accuracy

By the end of the year, we expect second-grade students to be able to:

- independently read aloud unfamiliar Level L* books with 90 percent or better accuracy of word recognition (self-correction allowed).

Fluency

By the end of the year, we expect second-grade students to be able to:

- independently read aloud from unfamiliar Level L books that they have previewed silently on their own, using intonation, pauses and emphasis that signal the meaning of text, and
- use the cues of punctuation—including commas, periods, question marks, and quotation marks—to guide them in getting meaning and fluently reading aloud.

Self-Monitoring and Self-Correcting Strategies

By the end of the year, we expect second-grade students to:

- know when they don't understand a paragraph and search for clarification clues within the text; and
- examine the relationship between earlier and later parts of a text and figure out how they make sense together.

cont.

---

*Level L books are markedly different from texts at lower levels. These books typically are longer chapter books with only a few illustrations that provide much less support for readers. The text size is smaller, and the word spacing is narrower.

Level L books feature more characters who are involved in more complex plots. The language structures are more sophisticated, detailed and descriptive. The vocabulary is challenging.

In general, Level L books require higher-level conceptual thinking for students to understand the subtleties of plot and character development. Students must sustain their reading over several days to finish the book. Most of the reading is done silently and independently, but some parts of the book may be read aloud for emphasis or interest. Group discussion may support readers during and after they read Level L books (New Standards Primary Literacy Committee, 1999, p. x).

FIGURE 2.2. Primary Literacy Standards for second grade.

From New Standards Primary Literacy Committee (1999, pp. 144–152). Copyright 1999 by the National Center on Education and the Economy and the University of Pittsburgh. Reprinted by permission.

Comprehension

By the end of second grade, we expect children to demonstrate their comprehension of a variety of narrative, literacy, functional and information texts that they read independently or with a partner, as well as texts that adults read to them.

For books that are read independently, including functional and informational texts, we expect children at the end of second grade to be able to do all of the things we expect of them in first grade, both orally and in writing. In addition, we expect them to:

- recognize and be able to talk about organizing structures;
- combine information from two different parts of the text;
- infer cause and effect relationships that are not stated explicitly;
- compare the observations of the author to their own observations when reading non-fiction texts; and
- discuss how, why and what-if questions about non-fiction texts.

The texts that adults read to second graders usually have more complex conceptual and syntactic features than the texts the children read independently, and this permits greater depth in the kinds of comprehension children can display. For texts we read to them, we expect children at the end of second grade to be able to do all of the things they can do for independently read texts. In addition, we expect them to:

- discuss or write about the themes of a book—what the "messages" of the book might be;
- trace characters and plots across multiple episodes, perhaps ones that are read on successive days; and
- relate later parts of a story to earlier parts, in terms of themes, cause and effect, etc.

FIGURE 2.2. *cont.*

ness. However, for those children who enter second grade as struggling readers, an assessment of phonemic awareness (which takes only a few minutes) will help teachers to understand these students' learning needs and to develop an effective instructional plan. (See Chapter 6 for tests of phonemic awareness.) Focused instruction in phonemic awareness makes a difference for students who demonstrate that they are not yet able to hear, segment, and blend sounds in words. Studies indicate that phonemic awareness training results in improvement in students' phonemic awareness, word reading, and spelling abilities (National Reading Panel Report, 2000).

Yopp (1992) identified five types of activities that support the development of phonemic awareness: sound matching, sound isolation, sound blending, sound substitution, and sound segmentation. Each of these types of activities represents a separate level of conceptual understanding, from the least to the most difficult.

There are many ways to develop these levels of understanding. Cunningham (2005) recommends that children be exposed to many books that contain rhyme, and suggests that teachers share texts in ways that cause children to think about the sounds of words. For example, she suggests having children clap or chime in on rhyming words. After reading and rereading a particular book several times, children can then follow the author's rhyming patterns and make up their own rhymes. Tasks such as these are appealing because in addition to developing phonemic awareness, they have the potential to cultivate a love of books and reading, as well as a love of particular authors. Cunningham suggests four simple steps by which to carry out her recommendations:

1. Pick a book with lots of rhymes and read it to the students several times.

2. Once children are familiar with the book, draw their attention to words that rhyme and ask them to identify the rhyming words and say them with you as you read.

3. Read the book again, this time stopping before the rhyming word and having children say the word.

4. Have children produce their own rhymes, using the pattern in the book as an exemplar.

Paying attention to rhyming words is likely to support the skills of sound matching and (perhaps) sound isolation but unlikely to develop the skills of sound segmenting, sound substitution, and sound blending. *Segmenting* requires that students "break apart" the sounds in a word by isolating each discrete sound they hear. *Sound substitution* requires the ability to isolate a sound, remove it, and replace it with a different sound. *Blending* requires the ability to put segmented sounds together to make a word. These skills are important for both reading and spelling words. A task commonly recommended for teaching sound segmentation, isolation, and blending skills is one that involves the use of Elkonin boxes. Rasinski and Padak (2001) explain:

> An Elkonin box is simply a series of boxes drawn on a sheet of paper, one for each phoneme in a given word. As students listen to words read by the teacher and hear discrete sounds, they push markers into the boxes, one marker for each sound. Later, as children become more familiar with written letters, they write individual letters or letter combinations that represent individual sounds in words. (p. 41)

Figures 2.3 and 2.4 provide examples of how children might represent the sounds they hear in Elkonin boxes. Notice that in Figure 2.4, the task has changed from one that requires students to use markers to represent sounds to one that

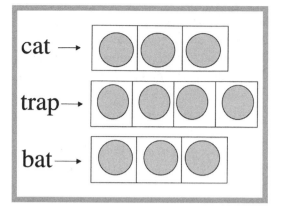

FIGURE 2.3. Examples of Elkonin boxes with chips.

requires the use of letters to represent sounds. This is an important difference because it changes the task from one that teaches only phonemic awareness to one that also teaches phonics. In the next section, we explain how these abilities differ and why we suggest that you plan to develop them together.

Phonics

We have defined phonemic awareness as the ability to recognize discrete sounds in words. As such, it is a task that can be taught without showing children any print at all. Phonics, however, is dependent on print; it is the ability to associate the sounds we hear in words with the letters that represent them. Although we believe that it is important for teachers to understand the differences between phonemic awareness and phonics, we also believe that it is important to pay attention to the conclusion drawn by the National Reading Panel that teaching phonemic awareness with print is more effective than teaching it without print. The authors of the National Reading Panel Report (2000) explain that use of print helps children to transfer phonemic awareness skills to reading and writing tasks. We like to think of tasks that are designed to develop both phonemic awareness and phonics as doing double duty—they are tasks that develop awareness of the sounds in language at the same time that they develop awareness of the letters that represent those sounds. In addition, tasks that are designed to focus on both phonemic awareness and phonics in a second-grade classroom are likely to meet the needs of a broader range of students—those who would benefit from the development of both abilities, and those who are "ready" for higher-level phonics skills.

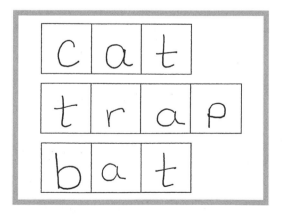

FIGURE 2.4. Examples of Elkonin boxes with letters.

In any discussion of phonics instruction, the so-called controversy about teaching phonics inevitably enters. Countless experts have weighed in on this issue, and there is substantial evidence to support the relationship between systematic instruction in phonics and children's success in learning to read (National Reading Panel Report, 2000). We find the explanation provided by Michael Graves, Connie Juel, and Bonnie Graves (2004) to be especially helpful in considering how the research evidence should influence classroom practice:

> Some children need less phonics instruction than others, and phonics instruction must always be kept in proper perspective—as a means to an end. Constructing meaning is the main goal of reading; and reading, writing, speaking, listening, and being read to must form the heart of the literacy curriculum. But for readers who have not yet mastered the code of written English, word recognition instruction—which includes phonics—plays an absolutely essential role. (p. 159)

What does this mean for the second-grade teacher? First, teachers must know how to determine what children already know about phonics and what they need to know to become better readers. (We provide suggestions for assessing students' word knowledge in Chapter 6.) Second, teachers need to know how to plan and guide instruction in the skills they determine children need. The word-study principles outlined by Graves et al. (2004) provide an especially useful framework for planning word-study instruction (Figure 2.5). In our work with classroom teachers, we have found that when they use these principles to guide their development of word-study lessons, the lessons comply with what we know about good teaching. That is, their lessons are responsive to children's needs; they engage children actively in the learning process; they engage children in thoughtful study and reflection, rather than rote learning; they integrate learning disciplines (in this case, reading and writing); and they focus on making meaning.

1. Start where the child is.

2. Make word study an active, decision-making process in which children classify words according to the similarity of their sounds and spelling patterns.

3. Base word study on contrasting words with different sounds or spelling patterns.

4. Help children understand how the writing system works.

5. Keep comprehension as the goal.

FIGURE 2.5. Word-study principles.

From Graves, Juel, and Graves (2004, p. 161). *Teaching reading in the 21st century* (3rd Ed.). Published by Allyn and Bacon. Copyright 2004 by Pearson Education, Inc. Reprinted by permission.

Implicit in these guidelines is an understanding that the teacher must engage in modeling and demonstration, guided practice, and independent practice of how to apply knowledge of each new phonic element to word reading. In addition, because many children struggle with blending sounds into words, teachers should provide many opportunities for children to observe and practice blending sounds into words that make sense (Graves et al., 2004).

Finally, although these principles provide general guidelines about *how* to teach, second-grade teachers also need to know *what* to teach. That is, what are the word parts that are useful to study and practice? There are many such lists available. For example, Cunningham (2005) identified 37 high-frequency phonograms especially helpful to young readers (Figure 2.6) and writers, and Rasinski and Padak (2001) provide a more extensive list (Appendix B). As children advance in second-grade reading, they begin to encounter longer and more complex words. To read these, they need to receive instruction in how to use common morphemes—meaning-bearing units—to "unlock the pronunciation, spelling, and meaning of polysyllabic words" (Cunningham, 2003, p. 72). Once again, Cunningham (2005) suggests a list of prefixes and suffixes that have especially high utility, "The Nifty Thrifty Fifty" (Figure 2.7).

Vocabulary

Vocabulary instruction can be divided into two types: activities that help children to acquire a sight vocabulary and activities that help children to acquire a meaning vocabulary. Sight vocabulary activities focus on helping children to develop rapid recognition of words that occur with high levels of frequency in the various texts that they read. Developing a large and appropriate sight vocabulary is important

---

37 high-frequency spelling patterns (with possible key words)

ack (black)	ap (cap)	est (nest)	ing (king)	at (hot)
ail (pail)	ash (trash)	ice (rice)	ink (pink)	lick (truck)
ain (train)	at (cat)	ide (bride)	ip (ship)	ug (bug)
ake (cake)	ate (skate)	ick (brick)	it (hit)	limp (jump)
ale (whale)	aw (claw)	ight (night)	ock (sock)	unk (skunk)
ame (game)	ay (tray)	ill (hill)	oke (Coke)	
an (pan)	eat (meat)	in (pin)	op (mop)	
ank (bank)	ell (shell)	ine (nine)	are (store)	

FIGURE 2.6. Common phonograms.

From Cunningham (2005). Published by Allyn and Bacon. Copyright 2005 by Pearson Education, Inc. Reprinted by permission.

The Nifty Thrifty Fifty

Word	Prefix	Suffix or ending	Word	Prefix	Suffix or ending
antifreeze	anti		international	inter	al
beautiful		ful (y-i)	invasion	in	sion
classify		ify	irresponsible	ir	ible
communities	com	es (y-i)	midnight	mid	
community	com		misunderstand	mis	
composer	com	er	musician		ian
continuous	con	ous	nonliving	non	ing (drop e)
conversation	con	tion	overpower	over	
deodorize	de	ize	performance	per	ance
different		ent	prehistoric	pre	ic
discovery	dis		prettier		er
dishonest	dis		rearrange	re	
electricity		ity	replacement	re	ment
employee	em	ee	richest		est
encouragement	en	ment	semifinal	semi	
expensive	ex	ive	signature		ture
forecast	fore		submarine	sub	
forgotten		en (double t)	supermarkets	super	s
governor		or	swimming		ing (double m)
happiness		ness (y-i)	transportation	trans	tion
hopeless		less	underweight	under	
illegal	il		unfinished	un	ed
impossible	im		unfriendly	un	ly
impression	im		unpleasant	un	ant
independence	in	ence	valuable		able (drop e)

FIGURE 2.7. Common prefixes and suffixes.

From Cunningham (2005, pp. 152–153). Published by Allyn and Bacon. Copyright 2005 by Pearson Education, Inc. Reprinted by permission.

because the ability to read words accurately and fluently allows children to focus their attention on making meaning as they read, rather than on decoding unknown words (LaBerge & Samuels, 1974). Developing a substantial meaning vocabulary is important because there is a strong relationship between vocabulary knowledge and reading comprehension (Freebody & Anderson, 1983).

Developing Sight Vocabulary

Children develop a rapid recognition of words from several activities. Perhaps the most important is the opportunity to read, read, read. The more children read, the greater the number of opportunities to encounter and practice high-frequency words. So a simple rule of thumb in the second-grade classroom is to make certain that children are given many opportunities each day to read and reread both familiar and unfamiliar texts. In addition to wide reading are other activities that help children develop rapid recognition of a large collection of words. One common practice is to have each child keep a word bank—a collection of words that either are instantly recognized by the child or are in the process of becoming instantly recognized (Rasinski & Padak, 2001). As such, the word bank functions both as a record of what the child knows and as a source of words that the child can use in various word-study activities: sorting by spellings, by meaning, by part of speech, and so forth. Word banks can take many forms: as small index cards filed within a file box; cards with punch holes that allow them to be hung on a ring; or envelopes of words filed alphabetically or by another useful category. Because word banks are only useful if students are given many opportunities to read and reread the words in thoughtful and productive ways, it is important that teachers consider word bank activities within the context of the word study principles cited earlier in this chapter.

In addition to individual word banks, teachers now commonly use word walls in classrooms. Word walls can have an array of different purposes but common to all is that they provide a place where children can access words that may be helpful to them as they read and write. Although word walls have the potential to support children's word learning, not all word walls are effective in meeting this goal. Cunningham (2005) draws a distinction between "having" a word wall and "doing" a word wall (p. 70). She explains that having a word wall might mean "putting words up somewhere in the room and telling children to use them" (p. 68), a strategy that may not be at all helpful to struggling readers. On the other hand, Cunningham explains, teachers who *do* a word wall:

➢ Are selective in choosing words, displaying those that are most commonly used in children's reading or writing.

➢ Add a limited number of words each week—as few as five additions.

➢ Position the word wall where children can see it and reproduce the words in a size and a color that are easily readable from various locations in the classroom.

➢ Provide many opportunities to review and practice the words on the wall.

➤ Hold children responsible for correct spelling of any words that are displayed on the word wall.

Developing Meaning Vocabulary

We recently met with teachers in a large, high-poverty, linguistically diverse urban school district for the first of six meetings on improving the instruction of reading in their schools. At the start of the opening conversation, we asked teachers to identify what they perceived to be their greatest challenges in improving the students' reading achievement. Without exception, every teacher said that the children lacked the vocabulary knowledge they needed to become proficient readers. These teachers' observations were remarkably consistent with numerous formal studies: Many studies indicate that one explanation for low levels of reading performance among English-language learners is inadequate English vocabulary (Garcia, 1991; Verhoeven, 1990); other studies indicate that children from higher socioeconomic groups (SES) know about twice as many words as their peers from lower socioeconomic groups, and these differences predict lower levels of reading performance not only at the end of first grade (Senechal & Cornell, 1993) but also at the end of their high school years (Cunningham & Stanovich, 1997).

Despite widespread recognition by teachers that many of their students lack sufficient vocabulary knowledge to succeed as readers and writers, "all available evidence indicates that there is little emphasis on the acquisition of vocabulary in school curricula" (Beck, McKeown, & Kucan, 2002, p. 2). Instead, vocabulary learning in classrooms is largely left to practices based on long-held beliefs: Children are given definitions of words in an often long list of unrelated words; children are taught to use the dictionary to find word meanings; or, children are expected to expand their vocabulary knowledge incidentally through wide reading. The problem with each of these techniques is that research indicates very little payoff, especially for children who lack the language awareness and knowledge to make their own connections between and among lists of new words. Especially worrisome is the expectation that children will "grow" their vocabularies through reading alone. Consider the conclusions drawn by María Carlo and her colleagues (2004):

> The probability of acquiring an unknown word incidentally through reading is only about 15%, which means the word would have to be encountered eight times to be learned with high probability. The probability of learning any word at a first encounter is lower for younger readers, for more difficult texts, and probably for students who have had no training in deriving meanings for unknown words. (p. 191)

It is difficult to overstate the potential harm that continuing to use such unsuccessful practices would do to the commonly stated goal of "leaving no child behind." In a recent chapter, Judith Scott (2004) responded to the evidence of low achievement and poor teaching practice with a "call to action, a call for teachers to actively and passionately embrace a curriculum that promotes accelerated and generative word knowledge for students who depend on schools and on teachers to teach them how to use words effectively" (p. 275). Similarly, Beck et al. (2002) argue that teachers must make effective vocabulary instruction a very high priority and that such instruction must be characterized by an approach that is "robust—vigorous, strong, and powerful in effect" (p. 2). Building on this work, Connie Juel and Rebecca Deffes (2004) suggest that teachers follow four steps to develop effective vocabulary instruction, particularly for young children with weak oral language skills:

1. Focus on words contextualized in literature, on words that are important to the text and useful to know in many situations, and on words that are uncommon in everyday language but recurrent in books.

2. Provide clear explanations and examples of word meanings in various contexts and provide opportunities for students to discuss, analyze, use, and compare the words in these contexts.

3. Furnish repeated occasions for students to hear words in varied contexts and to relate them to their own experiences and new knowledge.

4. Encourage students to use words in new contexts and discover other interesting words. (pp. 31–32)

A number of vocabulary learning practices have been found to be beneficial in improving children's word learning and also fit well within this lesson-planning framework. Two especially effective practices are semantic mapping and semantic feature analysis. The strategy of semantic mapping (Johnson & Pearson, 1984) uses a graphic organizer to help students represent and "unpack" the ideas associated with a particular word or concept. This strategy can be especially effective before reading, to help children access or build concept knowledge related to the text, and then after reading, to help children to connect new information or ideas to their existing knowledge. See, for example, the ideas recorded on the map displayed in Figure 2.8. Children contributed to this map before and after reading. The ideas recorded without underlining are those that the children shared before reading Byrd Baylor's (1976) *Hawk, I'm Your Brother*; the ideas underlined were offered after reading.

Another research-based strategy for helping students clarify their understanding of particular words and concepts is semantic feature analysis (Johnson & Pearson, 1984). As the term suggests, this task prompts children to think about the particular features of words and concepts; it can be used to lead even young children through a process of contrastive analysis. An example of semantic feature

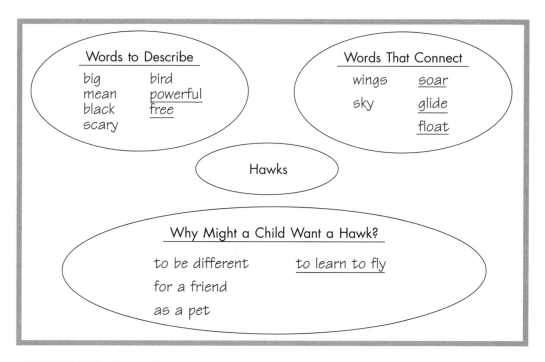

FIGURE 2.8. Semantic map.

analysis completed in a second-grade classroom is presented in Figure 2.9. After reading *Hawk, I'm Your Brother,* the children decided to explore the features of birds in greater depth. They used the feature analysis grid to consider the characteristics of different birds.

Semantic maps and semantic feature analysis can be very helpful in carrying out step 2 in the sequence of steps outlined by Juel and Deffes. But notice that if these strategies are used by themselves and without explicit attention by teachers to the other steps in this list of guidelines, many children will not receive the kind of instruction that is likely to make a difference in their vocabulary learning. There is no quick fix for the gap that many children experience in vocabulary knowledge. Rather, effective vocabulary instruction requires intensive, thoughtful, and well-planned teaching. Implicit in this statement is an understanding that teachers know a good deal about word learning. Judith Scott (2004) explains that teachers who know how to teach vocabulary effectively understand some fundamental ideas, among them:

1. Word learning is multidimensional. That is, children must learn that different words have different meanings in different contexts.
2. Word learning is incremental and takes place in many steps over time.

Birds	Small	Large	Powerful	Gentle	Tame	Wild	Many	Few
Hawk	–	+	+	–	–	+	–	+
Robin	+	–	–	–	–	+	+	–
Parakeet	+	+	–	–	+	+	+	–
Goldfinch	+	–	–	+	–	+	+	–
Robin	+	–	–	+	–	+	+	–
Sparrow	+	–	–	+	–	+	+	–

FIGURE 2.9. Semantic feature analysis.

3. Different words require different types of instruction. That is, some can be easily connected to known words or concepts, while others require the development of new ideas and understandings.

4. Traditional dictionaries are poor tools for learning the meanings of words.

5. Word consciousness and generative knowledge about words are useful and important. (p. 278)

Of all of these ideas, an understanding of the concept of *word consciousness* may be the most fundamental to the routine practice of effective instruction in vocabulary. That is, when vocabulary learning tasks are (1) active and interactive, (2) require students to consider words from a variety of different perspectives, (3) ask students to connect words to what they know and experience, and (4) encourage students to use words in an array of contexts (both serious and playful), then students actually begin to think about and look out for words and ways to use them in the course of their daily activities. It is the development of this disposition—referred to as word consciousness by Scott and others (e.g., Anderson & Nagy, 1992, Graves & Watts-Taffe, 2002)—that experts believe will ultimately be consequential in helping *all* children acquire both the depth and breadth of vocabulary knowledge that will propel them to higher levels of accomplishment in reading comprehension and in all areas of the curriculum.

Fluency

Nancy Roser and her colleagues (2003) defined fluency as "reading with accuracy, adequate rate, and (for oral reading, at least) prosody—or the musicality that includes appropriate stress, pitch, and juncture" (p. 42). The understanding that reading fluency is a critical factor in the development of reading comprehension was largely established two decades ago, but it received renewed attention following the National Reading Panel Report (2000). As a result of its renewed popularity, researchers and teachers have focused more attention on the types of instructional practices that are beneficial to developing fluency and, in particular, on practices that are appropriate for use with children in classrooms rather than with children in individual, tutorial settings (Kuhn, 2003). Strategies for developing fluency are especially important to second-grade teachers, because it is during this school year when fluency becomes a particular area of focus. Yet several experts note that, despite its importance, many teachers lack an understanding of the particular strategies that are appropriate for facilitating fluency development (Allington, 1983a; Kuhn, 2003; Roser et al., 2003)

As with other areas of reading improvement, the first rule of thumb in supporting children's development of fluency is to provide abundant amounts of reading time for them. We know that fluency is especially supported when children are engaged in rereading familiar text (Samuels, 1979); one challenge teachers face is to design contexts that are at once motivational and also provide some form of external monitoring. Paired rereadings (Koskinen & Blum, 1986) provide a setting in which children can read together, alternating pages. With training from the teacher, students learn to act as a coach to their partner, assisting with unknown words and providing positive feedback. Although Koskinen and Blum recommend a detailed system for listening and recording children's oral reading performance, in many classrooms teachers use it far less formally, simply pairing students daily, or even several times a day, to read and reread shared texts.

A second strategy that is especially suited for use with small groups of children is Readers' Theatre. Roser et al. (2003) defined Readers' Theatre as "an interpretive reading activity in which readers use their voices to bring characters to life" (p. 43). Unlike repeated readings, which typically emphasize rate and accuracy, Readers' Theatre "focuses on how meaningfully a text is interpreted orally" (Roser et al., p. 43). Roser and her colleagues (Martinez, Roser, & Strecker, 1998/1999) examined the effects of Readers' Theatre on the reading fluency of second graders and found significant gains in fluency as well as in children's motivation and engagement in reading practice and performance. In Chapter 3, we return to the practice of Readers' Theatre and other activities that promote fluency and provide some explicit ideas for implementation.

Comprehension

In their study of highly effective classroom teachers at each grade level, Cathy Collins Block, Margaret Oakar, and Nicholas Hurt (2002) reported that excellent second-grade teachers are "master demonstrators" (p. 190) who dedicate substantial time to helping students make sense of both classroom text and classroom talk throughout the course of the school day. In particular, excellent second-grade teachers (1) help children develop background knowledge through "masterful think alouds" (p. 188); (2) they listen and respond in ways that stimulate "substantive conversations" (p. 188); and (3) plan and implement lessons that present concepts in ways that students have not otherwise heard or seen.

In her study of the nature of instruction provided to children as they progressed from kindergarten to second grade, Diane Barone (2003/2004) also found that the instruction offered to second graders was substantially different from the instruction they received in their earlier school years, particularly as it related to reading comprehension. Unlike their teaching peers in the earlier grades, the second-grade teachers Barone studied employed strategies that facilitated children's reading comprehension by making "academic conversation the centerpiece of instruction for all students including ELL [English language learner] students" (p. 990). In addition, Barone reported that second-graders encountered more diverse texts, as teachers used both narrative and expository text as part of their standard curriculum.

What does it mean to be a "master demonstrator" or to make academic conversation "the centerpiece" of instruction? Why are these characteristics central to a discussion about comprehension? What would your classroom look like if you did this? To answer these questions, we have organized our thoughts into three categories: skillful and strategic teaching; interesting, motivating, and diverse texts; and purposeful and meaningful contexts.

Skillful and Strategic Teaching

Among the most persistent findings of the last three decades of reading research is the evidence that "good readers are very active and strategic as they read" (Block & Pressley, 2003, p. 114). What do we know about instructional practices that lead even struggling readers to become active and strategic? At its core, such instruction is based on a model of teaching that includes demonstration, guided practice, and independent practice. Described by David Pearson and Margaret Gallagher (1983) as a gradual release of responsibility model, this approach to teaching is based on theoretical evidence that learners acquire new information in contexts in which they first observe the teacher complete a task, then complete a task with the teacher, and then, as their level of expertise increases, they are presented with opportunities to practice the task on their own. This instructional approach is often referred to as one form of instructional scaffolding. It is largely based on the cognitive learning theory of Lev Vygotsky (1978), who claimed that "using imitation, children are capable of doing much more in collective activity or under the guidance of adults" (p. 88) than they would be able to do on their own. We especially like Camille Blachowicz's and Donna Ogle's (2001) explanation of scaffolded instruction:

> Anyone who has ever taught a child to ride a bike knows what "scaffolded" instruction and learning is. You don't give the child 10 minutes of skill lessons on pedaling, 10 minutes on balancing, 10 minutes on ringing the bell, and so on; you put the child on the bike so he or she can get the "feel" of the whole activity. The goal is to provide just enough help so that the child can succeed.
>
> But you don't just go sit on the porch and have a cool drink while the child tries to ride. Rather, you run alongside the bike at first (or use training wheels) and hold on, letting go when the child is riding well, catching on when support is needed. The learner is put on a bike of the right size, set down to practice in a safe spot, and given praise for every little thing he or she learns. This is scaffolded instruction. (p. 29)

In the context of teaching reading comprehension, excellent teachers use the gradual release of responsibility model to help students to acquire a repertoire of strategies that are associated with good reading. Although different experts offer slightly different lists of strategies, some are common to all. Block and Pressley (2003) identify the following as the most commonly taught comprehension processes:

➢ Prediction

➢ Questioning

➢ Imagery

➢ Relating prior knowledge

➢ Monitoring

➢ Seeking clarification

➢ Summarizing

Block and Pressley (2003) explain that the skillful teacher introduces one strategy at a time, modeling and demonstrating through read-alouds and think-alouds, gradually demanding more of the students as they work collaboratively through a text. As students demonstrate that they are successfully using the first strategy, the teacher introduces a second strategy and demonstrates how a capable reader uses the two processes together. Introduction and practice of the full repertoire of comprehension strategies is typically spread out across the school year. As students encounter reading materials with different text structures, the skillful teacher steps back to the demonstration phase of instruction and explicitly explains and demonstrates how students might use the comprehension strategy to help them construct meaning as they read.

In addition to providing students with explicit instruction in an array of reading strategies, effective teachers also provide explicit instruction about text structures and the ways in which children should examine and use text structure to help them as they read. A popular instructional strategy is story mapping (Pearson & Johnson, 1984), a practice based on evidence that good readers use narrative text structure to help them predict, organize, and recall story events (Mandler & Johnson, 1977; Stein & Glenn, 1979). Excellent second-grade teachers also use some form of mapping or graphic organizers to help students access background knowledge and monitor their comprehension of nonfiction texts. However, since nonfiction texts structures are more varied than story structure, teachers must introduce students to an array of organizational plans, including description, comparison–contrast, problem–solution, cause–effect, and sequence.

Finally, there are many approaches to helping students learn to exercise their repertoire of reading strategies in effective and efficient ways. One that is especially useful to young readers is KWL (Ogle, 1986). This strategy engages children before reading by eliciting and discussing what students already know (K) and what they want to know (W) about a focal topic, and then, after reading, by eliciting what they have learned (L). The structure of a KWL chart (see photograph in Chapter 6, p. 118) provides a place where students can graphically represent their ideas; the chart then serves as a resource for discussion, conversation, and note taking during and after reading. In a recent review of the effects of KWL, Hefflin and Hartman (2002) concluded that it affects student comprehension in a "marked way" (p. 205). (For a more in-depth description of KWL, see Blachowicz & Ogle, 2001.)

Much like vocabulary instruction, comprehension instruction is successful when teachers emphasize the cognitive and metacognitive processes that good readers use. In short, in addition to asking children *what* they understand a selection to be about, effective teachers also ask students to explain *how* they constructed their understanding.

Interesting, Motivating, and Diverse Texts

In answer to the question, *What types of literature are important to use?*, Douglas Fisher, James Flood, and Diane Lapp (2003) suggested that teachers' choices be guided by four criteria: (1) high literary quality, (2) interesting and engaging aesthetic qualities, (3) concepts and ideas that are of high interest to students, and (4) text that leads children to unique discoveries. Our visits to second-grade classrooms convince us that these criteria are well known to teachers, and that teachers consistently attend to them in the books they choose to read aloud, to display, and to make available to students for self-selected reading. However, we are less certain that teachers consider these criteria when they choose books for instructional reading, and in particular, when they choose books for use in small guided reading groups. Our observations indicate that many of the books that are now commonly referred to as "leveled texts" (Fountas & Pinnell, 1996) vary substantially in literary quality from those that are used for teacher read-alouds or for independent reading. As a consequence, the texts that typically serve as the basis for students' introduction to, and first experience using, a new comprehension strategy may lack the qualities that we know engage children in careful reading and thoughtful reflection, and as such, they may provide a poor or insufficient context for instruction. Teachers can guard against this downfall by applying the criteria for selecting good books not only to the books they choose for reading aloud or for children's independent reading, but also to the books that they use in all forms of instructional reading groups.

In addition to unevenness in the literary quality of the instructional texts assigned to students, recent studies have indicated that children in the early grades primarily read narrative texts (Duke, 2000a, 2000b). The emphasis on reading and responding to stories has raised concern that children are not being adequately prepared for the type of reading that will predominate as they enter grade 4 and beyond. As a result, second-grade teachers are now expected to incorporate substantially more nonfiction texts within their reading curriculum. Providing students texts that are deliberately diverse in text structure is a positive development, but in order for children to successfully comprehend expository texts, teachers must also bring to these texts new instructional strategies. That is, just as teaching story structure is now common in most second-grade classrooms, teaching nonfiction structure (e.g., comparison–contrast, description, cause–effect) must also become commonplace.

Purposeful and Meaningful Contexts

The quality of the instructional context is cited by many as a critical factor in providing effective instruction in reading comprehension. In their analysis of evidence-based instruction of reading comprehension, Catherine Snow and Anne Sweet (2002) identify three factors that are particularly important in creating a context in which children become good comprehenders: (1) opportunities for student choices, (2) challenging tasks, and (3) collaborative learning. Why might these particular factors influence levels of reading achievement? We believe it is because each prompts children to engage in important cognitive processes. Consider, for example, the thinking process children might use when choosing books for independent reading. First, they are prompted to think about their reading interests and to seek books that match their interests. Next, their choices are also likely to engage them in evaluation: Do they like the book they chose? Is it interesting to them? Should they keep this book or find another? If they choose to find another, how will they find one that is a better match than this one? The simple task of selecting a book can potentially engage students in a series of decision-making exercises.

Similarly, challenging tasks are likely to provoke thought and cause children to engage actively in problem solving and critical thinking. These learning dispositions result in higher levels of engagement and, as a direct consequence, higher levels of achievement (Guthrie & Wigfield, 2000). Recognizing the importance of challenging contexts is especially important because of the evidence that suggests that lower-performing readers are often placed in contexts that lack cognitive challenge (Allington, 1991). The consequence of continuing this practice of providing struggling readers with low-level comprehension tasks is likely to be continued low-performance rates for children who are most dependent on high-quality instruction.

Finally, collaborative learning contexts build on the evidence that learning is largely a social process, and that social interaction related to text and text comprehension demands that students learn to articulate their understanding of what they have read and justify and defend their point of view. Contexts in which children are provided with opportunities for peer-led discussions are especially consistent with these ideas. The organization of students into literature circles (Short & Klassen, 1993) is a common practice. In her second-grade classroom, McCormack (1997) used a procedure she dubbed "Take Five" because of its five components: (1) get ready, (2) read, (3) reread, (4) respond, and (5) react. Within this model, the learning context may vary from step to step. That is, in the initial steps (get ready, read, reread), the teacher may facilitate the activities, whereas in the later steps (respond, react), the children may work within peer-led discussion groups. In reviewing the evidence she gathered as children worked within the Take Five model, McCormack found that these youngsters had the ability to choose their own topics and themes when talking about literature. Perhaps most important, the children raised questions and introduced themes that she would not have considered if she had led the discussion. In addition, she found that children had high expectations of each other. That is, following what they had seen their teacher do in earlier lessons, they demanded that their peers support their point of view using both the text and their own experiences. Finally, she found not only that small, peer-led groups gave more students the opportunity to contribute their ideas to the group discussion, but also that at times the strongest voices and opinions were those of students who rarely spoke in whole-class discussions. In Chapter 3 we return to this practice and provide additional examples of how effective teachers incorporate literature circles into their weekly instructional routines.

Writing

Throughout most of this chapter, we have addressed an array of factors as they relate to the teaching of reading. In fact, a great deal of the information that we have shared so far also relates to writing. For example, as we explained in the section on the development of phonemic awareness, students' ability to hear, segment, and blend sounds in words is fundamental to their ability to write and spell words. Similarly, children's understanding of letter–sound association—the skill of phonics—is used for decoding (reading) words and is also fundamental to the process of encoding words (more commonly known as spelling).

In our discussion of vocabulary, we emphasized the importance of vocabulary knowledge to reading comprehension. Vocabulary knowledge is also central to written composition. The more words children know, and the more they know *about* those words, the more precise their writing. In our discussion of comprehension, we emphasized the importance of teaching students about narrative and expository text structures to help them make predictions before reading, organize information as they read, and then recall, reflect, and respond after reading. These same text structures are used by writers as they plan, draft, and revise their writing. Just as the types of texts we provide for our young readers are central to their interest, engagement, and motivation for reading, these same texts can motivate, engage, and serve as exemplars for students in their writing efforts. Finally, in the same ways that purposeful and meaningful contexts provide beneficial settings for readers, writers, too, are supported by contexts in which they have choice, challenge, and opportunities to collaborate and share with their classmates.

How do you use these understandings to plan and implement a sound writing program for your second graders? Karen Bromley (2003) suggests five guidelines by which to shape your planning:

1. Work with your colleagues to establish school-wide or grade-level writing goals.

2. Create a learning environment that provides writing tools, sufficient time to write, and models of good writing.

3. Provide students with direct instruction in composition and the conventions of writing.

4. Give students opportunities to makes choices about writing topics, writing purposes, and writing audiences.

5. Use writing to help students construct meaning across the curriculum.

Implicit within these guidelines is an understanding that the underlying instructional approach to writing is a process approach in which children are given instruction in how to plan, draft, revise, edit, and publish their writing.

Motivation and Interest

When all is said and done, the need to develop children's motivation and interest in reading may be the single most important task facing the teacher. We have a substantial body of evidence supporting the important role of motivation: Positive literacy motivation correlates with higher levels of achievement, deeper cognitive processing, and greater conceptual understanding (Gambrell, 2004). But we also have plain and simple common sense: If we help children develop a love of reading, they will be more likely to choose to read, and the more they choose to read, the better they will likely read. What do we know about learning contexts that motivate children to read and write? Linda Gambrell (2004) outlined five characteristics. (Notice the congruence between these ideas and previous descriptions of contexts that support high achievement in reading.)

1. Classrooms that have an abundance of high-quality, high-interest books support sustained reading.

2. Children's self-selection of reading material is strongly correlated with motivation to read.

3. Providing students with uninterrupted and extended time to engage in reading correlates with motivation to read.

4. Having opportunities to discuss what they have read with their peers correlates with motivation to read.

5. Literacy activities that are connected to students' own lives and their cultural identities correlate with motivation to read.

We hope that you are struck by the realization that creating a learning context is not difficult and does not differ at all from the other tenets of effective instruction. Rather, what we hope is evident throughout this description of evidence-based instruction in reading and writing is substantial overlap in the teaching actions that lead children to experience success as they work on various aspects of literacy learning.

MAKING SENSE OF THE EVIDENCE

So far in this chapter, we have examined what children need to know, and we have taken a brief look at some of the instructional practices that help children achieve the benchmarks expected of them. As you begin to think about how you might operationalize these benchmarks in your own teaching, we would like to emphasize a point that we believe is critically important to the teaching decisions you make: Understanding how to teach in ways that optimize children's opportunities to learn is as important as knowing what teach. That is, research has shown consistently that teachers using the same curriculum or program often produce different learning outcomes, and the differences have been attributed to variations in teaching practices (Allington & Nowak, 2004; Bond & Dykstra, 1997; National Clearinghouse for Comprehensive School Reform, 2001).

Studies (e.g., Taylor & Pearson, 2002; Knapp, 1995; Pressley, Allington, Wharton-McDonald, Block, & Morrow, 2001) have indicated that teachers in classrooms where children are excelling in reading and writing share a core group of common and consistent instructional practices. This is true even for students who typically are expected to experience more failure in reading, that is, children who are challenged by both poverty and English language learning. Most (though not all) of these practices were identified as we discussed each of the essential literacy domains in this chapter; those not addressed here are discussed in later chapters. Here we draw these ideas together in a single list of claims that we think is useful as a framework to guide instructional planning:

1. Explicit instruction in phonemic awareness and alphabet knowledge supports acquisition of decoding skills (National Reading Panel Report, 2000).

2. Systematic instruction in phonics, in conjunction with coaching children to use decoding skills while reading authentic and meaningful texts, correlate with higher levels of reading achievement (Cunningham, 2003; National Reading Panel Report; Taylor & Pearson, 2002).

3. Providing time and experiences that support the development of reading fluency, including the ability to read words quickly, accurately, and expressively,

supports higher levels of reading achievement, in general, and reading comprehension, in particular (Kuhn, 2003; LaBerge & Samuels, 1974; National Reading Panel Report, 2000; Samuels, 1979; O'Shea, Sindelar, & O'Shea, 1985).

4. Direct and "robust" (Beck et al., 2002. p. 2) vocabulary instruction advances children's knowledge of word meanings and reading comprehension (Nagy, 1997; Scott, 2004).

5. Explicit instruction in comprehension strategies within the context of comprehension tasks that require higher level thinking result in higher-levels of reading achievement for students across grade levels and for students with varied learning profiles (Alvarez & Mehan, 2004; Baker & Allington, 2003; Barrerra & Jiménez, 2002; Englert & Dunsmore, 2002; Taylor & Pearson, 2002).

6. Instruction that is strategic—that is, instruction that is embedded within meaningful texts and includes direct explanation and modeling, teacher-guided practice, and meaningful and repeated opportunities for independent practice—contributes to higher levels of reading achievement (Block & Pressley, 2003; Pearson & Gallagher, 1983; Pressley et al., 1992).

7. The quality and quantity of the texts available to students correlate with higher levels of motivation and engagement in reading; students must have texts that are appropriate to their ages, interests, reading levels, cultures, and language (Worthy & Roser, 2004); they must also have such texts in sufficient quantity, referred to by Worthy and Roser (2004) as "flood ensurance" (p. 179).

8. Time to read for both instructional and recreational purposes contributes to higher levels of reading achievement (Anderson, 1996; Anderson, Wilson, & Fielding, 1988; Elley, 1996).

9. Grouping practices that allow all students access to the same rigorous curriculum and also provide opportunities for students to learn from texts that are appropriate to individual needs correlate with higher levels of reading achievement (Alvarez & Mehan, 2004; Cunningham, Hall, & Defee, 1991; Hall & Cunningham, 1996; Taylor & Pearson, 2002).

10. Instructional practices that have been proven effective for native English speakers work equally well with English-language learners (Bernhardt, 2000; Brisk & Harrington, 2000; Fitzgerald, 1995; Fizgerald & Nobbit, 1999).

11. Effective home–school collaboration programs correlate with higher rates of reading achievement (Epstein, 2001; Jordan, Snow, & Porche, 2000; Morrow & Young, 1997; Taylor & Pearson, 2002).

12. Assessment that is systematic, curriculum related, and classroom based correlates with higher levels of reading achievement (Taylor & Pearson, 2002).

LOOKING BACKWARD AND FORWARD

We began this chapter by presenting second-grade goals and benchmarks, and we related these to seven important areas of literacy research and theory: phonemic awareness, phonics, vocabulary, fluency, comprehension, writing, and motivation and interest. In each case, we presented a brief summary of the evidence that leads to claims that these abilities are essential to successful achievement in reading and writing. We also provided a few examples of the types of teaching strategies that are consistent with the evidence.

In the next chapter we turn to the evidence related to the characteristics of classroom environments in which children excel in learning to read and write. We describe what we know about classroom contexts that support literacy learning and how typical second-grade teachers use the evidence to arrange their classrooms and to develop classroom literacy routines. Then we visit the classroom of Pat Arterberry, a veteran teacher in New Bedford, Massachusetts, to observe the ways in which she translates the research evidence into sound classroom practice.

Try It Out

■ Consider the standards and benchmarks presented in this chapter for second-grade readers and consider the ways you presently teach children to read and write. In what ways are your practices likely to advance your students' progress toward these goals? Also consider goals and benchmarks that you might need to address more fully. Would you like to improve the ways you teach and support children's learning in particular areas? Which of the ideas presented in this chapter might help you address those areas of need? Try one out and share your reflections with a teaching colleague.

CHAPTER 3

SETTING UP THE CLASSROOM ENVIRONMENT FOR LITERACY

n Chapter 2 we explained and discussed the evidence base that underlies the ways in which excellent teachers frame instruction to optimize the learning opportunities of every child. Our focus was on teaching actions and behaviors. In this chapter we continue to address factors that influence children's literacy learning, but this time we focus on the ways in which excellent teachers arrange the learning environment. We have organized this chapter into two major sections: The first section describes the characteristics of an effective physical environment; the second section addresses the types of reading and writing routines that are likely to increase children's opportunities to learn.

CHARACTERISTICS OF AN EFFECTIVE PHYSICAL ENVIRONMENT FOR LEARNING

Beginning readers thrive in an environment that is abundant with print and ample opportunities to read, write, listen, and talk (Morrow & Gambrell, 2000). To support the literacy learning of all students, excellent second-grade teachers create classroom environments in which literacy is not only taught but also practiced in ways that convey to children that reading and writing are activities that are valued both for learning and for recreation and pleasure. How teachers arrange furniture and materials in classrooms influences the ways children use and share what they read and what they write.

What Should a Second-Grade Classroom Look Like?

The ways in which a teacher arranges her classroom speak volumes to children about the teacher's beliefs regarding reading and writing and her expectations of how her students will use reading and writing in the course of their daily activities. A thoughtful classroom arrangement can optimize opportunities to learn by minimizing transition time from one activity to the next, by providing easy access to learning resources, and by positioning children so that they can readily interact with their peers.

Excellent teachers begin by giving careful consideration to the arrangement of desks. One of the first questions a novice teacher asks is: "Should I arrange my desks in rows or in clusters?" To answer the question, the thoughtful teacher steps back and considers the learning implications of the various desk configurations. If we are committed to a classroom where children (1) share their ideas before, during, and after reading; (2) collaborate together to plan their writing; and (3) are allowed to engage in peer talk, which is considered an opportunity to use and practice language so that oral proficiency gets better and better each day—then having desks arranged so that they can easily share and interact is important. Positioning desks in clusters promotes conversation, collaboration, and interaction among the students—all characteristics of student behaviors in classrooms in which children excel in reading and writing (Bromley, 2003; Gambrell, 2004; Morrow & Asbury, 2003).

In addition, there should be a space within the classroom where the teacher can meet quietly and privately with an individual child or a small group of children. We recommend setting aside a corner of the classroom for the teacher's desk or for a small table and chairs, where private meetings can be held.

Next, organizing the room into focal areas for specific purposes helps to support learning routines. For example, excellent second-grade teachers designate areas for class meetings, whole-group instruction, as well as small-group work. Shelves, rugs, and other furniture can be used to designate such areas.

Excellent teachers use wall space for meaningful displays of information that help children learn. For example, in one of our classroom visits, we saw a display titled "As I Write." Each of the cards on the board reminded students of steps to follow as they write. In another, a teacher used a wall display to prompt children to think and write about an upcoming topic in social studies or science. She posted a chart that said: "Next week we are going to read about life in ponds and streams. On this chart, list words that name things you have seen in a pond or a stream." In yet another classroom, a teacher posts a "question of the day" right near the entry to the classroom; the question relates to a topic that children will encounter that day. The daily routine is very clear: Children enter the classroom, read the question, and respond accordingly. In preparation for a unit on the sun and the stars, the question of the day might be: What words would you use to describe the sky? Students record their responses on a chart or easel paper, and they are encouraged to read what others have written. The teacher then uses the page that displays their responses as she begins her discussion of the focal topic. Such displays should change frequently, reflecting the curriculum of the day or week.

Similarly, word walls, now a common display in many second-grade classrooms, should be more than displays of words. You may recall that in Chapter 2, we discussed the difference between "doing" and "having" a word wall (Cunningham, 2003). This is an important distinction that determines whether a display is simply aesthetically pleasing or instructionally beneficial. In short, word walls should be positioned where children can readily refer to them when reading or writing, and they should represent children's emerging word knowledge, changing as known words are removed and new words are added.

The central point that we are trying to convey about the ways teachers arrange furniture and wall displays is that the arrangements should not be simply decorative. Rather, by their very nature, the arrangements should invite children to read, think, write, and talk—and thereby increase their opportunities to engage in literate behaviors.

How Should I Organize the Classroom Library?

Excellent second-grade teachers display books in spaces throughout their classrooms (Morrow, 2002), and they also designate particular spaces as classroom libraries. Thoughtfully organized classroom libraries offer students opportunities to learn strategies for choosing books, to sample books related to familiar and unfamiliar topics, and to read and reread alone or with a peer. Research suggests that children prefer to choose books from classroom libraries rather than the school library, public libraries, or bookstores (Worthy & McCool, 1996).

As I write chart.

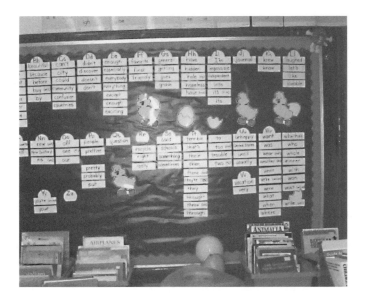

Word wall.

In order to set up a high-quality library in your second-grade classroom, two factors are critical: organization of the space and careful selection of books and other materials.

Organizing the Library Space

Many literacy experts have written about effective ways to organize classroom library space. The guidelines that follow represent a composite of ideas drawn from many sources, including Fractor, Woodruff, Martinez, and Teale (1993); Morrow (1993); Morrow (2002); and Lapp, Flood, and Roser (2000).

➤ Choose a quiet, well-lit space large enough for at least five children to sit comfortably. Soft chairs, pillows, and rugs approximate the ways many people position themselves for reading outside of school and encourage extended reading for pleasure.

➤ Make the library a focal point of your classroom. By doing so you will convey to your students that the classroom library is a highly valued place, and that reading is an important activity.

➤ Have at least seven or eight books per child in your classroom collection. If your classroom library is too small, consider ways to expand it at little or no cost. For example, many school or community librarians will allow teachers to borrow a sizable number of books on a monthly basis, changing the collection so that the classroom library is constantly being "refreshed." You might also check into low-priced classroom-library collections available from publishers or bookstores. But be careful—be picky about the books that are offered to you at low prices. You are better off having fewer high-quality literature books that will truly engage children in the joy of reading than a large number of books that fails to convince emerging and developing readers that reading is fun or worthwhile!

➢ Choose a variety of ways to display your books. Display a major portion of the books on accessible shelves of appropriate height for second graders. These books can be shelved with the spines visible so that a greater number of books fits into a smaller space. However, books should also be displayed so that children can see the covers, especially when books about a particular theme or concept being studied are featured. Open-faced bookshelves, plastic crates, or swiveling wire racks can be used so that the covers are visible. In addition, choosing different books to feature "cover out" each month, including books of all genres, themes, and topics, can motivate and stimulate new interests in reading.

➢ Organize books by category, using color codes or symbols, and shelve or group these books together. Books can be categorized in many ways. For example, organizing by literary genre can help us respond to children who say, "I really like mysteries" or "I really like stories about real people and events." Organizing by author can be useful when we are helping children to explore different writing styles. Organizing by theme or concept helps us to support content-area or thematic-based learning; and organizing by topic can help us respond to children's special interests.

➢ Organize books by level of reading difficulty. This method of organization is especially useful for helping children to choose books that they can read with relative ease. A commonly used system for leveling books is that developed by Fountas and Pinnell (1996), which sorts according to a lettered hierarchy of reading difficulty. Providing children with books that are easy to read is a practice that supports their development of reading accuracy and fluency (Juel & Roper/Schneider, 1985). However, as with any other practice, teachers must be careful not to overinterpret the research. Instructionally, it is important to provide children with many opportunities to read and reread texts that are easy, and to provide opportunities for students to apply the reading strategies they are acquiring. Recreationally, however, children's self-selection of books should not be limited by designated levels. Children should be given the opportunity to choose books that engage them socially, emotionally, and cognitively. These may be different from those that appear in the various leveled bins.

Cozy book corner.

Once the space and shelves are organized, the next task is choosing appropriate books for your students. Second-grade teachers know that their students are naturally motivated to read and are curious about the world around them; in fact it is quite a challenge to provide enough high-quality books for second-grade students to read and enjoy.

Book display.

Book display.

Selecting Books

There are so many factors to consider in choosing books for the classroom library; luckily, there are also many sources to help you to make choices. Here, our purpose is only to provide some very basic guidelines to help you get started. In Chapter 8 we recommend sources for finding the books you need.

In Chapter 2 we cited the work of Douglas Fisher, James Flood, and Diane Lapp (2003) and noted the suggestion of these educators that teachers' book choices be guided by four criteria: (1) high literary quality; (2) interesting and engaging aesthetic qualities; (3) concepts and ideas that are of high interest to students; and (4) content that leads children to new and unique discoveries. These are basic criteria for the selection of any classroom texts, whether intended for instructional or recreational reading. In addition to meeting these criteria, a classroom library should maintain a balance of narrative and expository texts with themes and topics relevant to both boys and girls in second grade. All genres (e.g., realistic fiction, historical fiction, fantasy, traditional tales poetry, and informational text) should be represented through both pictures books and chapter books.

An additional consideration may be the developmental profiles typical of young children. You may recall that in Chapter 1 we introduced Will and discussed the ways in which his writing and reading interests were related to developmental theory. Just as we used theories about child development to understand Will as an individual child, we can also use these theories as a basis on which to predict the interests and motivations of many of the children in second-grade classrooms. For example, as we noted in Chapter 1 regarding the student Will's reading interests, for children in the age range of second graders, Huck, Heckler, Hickman, and Keifer (2003) recommend books about the warmth and security of family relationships. They explain that books about families that resemble children's own can provide emotional comfort, while books about families different from their own can provide vicarious experiences that help them to develop understanding and empathy toward those who are not like themselves. Huck et al. also use developmental theory to predict that children in this age group may be working out the differences between reality and fantasy, and they suggest that fanciful books can support this development. They note that as this stage of development many children especially enjoy stories in which a major element is magic, and so you might select books of this type for your classroom library. Fairy tales, fables, and other traditional tales offer simple fantasy plots, and contemporary fantasy novels offer longer and more complex plot development. Children in this age range are also developing their sense of humor. Picture books and poetry that are whimsical and humorous are among their favorites. Second graders also show a strong and growing sense of justice and they demand the application of rules, sometimes regardless of circumstances. Realistic fiction, historical fiction, and some fantasy provide themes of social fairness and peer-group acceptance.

You might also return to the Primary Literacy Standards (Appendix A) to guide and inform your classroom library selections. For example, "Reading Standard 3: Reading Habits," indicates that by the end of second grade, children should be able to:

➢ Read and understand chapter books.

➢ Read and compare multiple books by the same author.

➢ Read responses to literature (e.g., book blurbs and reviews).

➢ Read poetry and plays.

➢ Read the writing of their classmates, including pieces compiled in class books.

➢ Compare books by different authors in the same genre.

➢ Discuss recurring themes across works.

As you choose books for your classroom library, it is important to provide choices that will enable children to have reading experiences that, in combination with good teaching, are likely to advance them toward these standards.

As a final thought about book selection, we know that in any second-grade classroom, children's instructional and independent reading abilities vary widely. The books in the classroom library should reflect this range, so that every child has access to a range of books that offers both ease of reading and challenge.

Selecting Other Print and Nonprint Materials

In addition to books, second-grade students need ample opportunities to interact with other forms of printed and nonprinted materials from a wide variety of genres and categories. Introducing children to diverse types of texts provides experience that supports "wide reading," that is, reading that extends across a variety of genres and topics. Research suggests that wide reading contributes to fluency, strategy use, increased vocabulary, and greater background knowledge (Anderson, Wilson, & Fielding, 1988; Anderson, 1996; Stanovich, 1986). Well-equipped classroom libraries should include magazines, newspapers, videos, and software that introduce children to the different ways in which good readers acquire information and build funds of knowledge. Excellent second-grade teachers provide copies of age-appropriate magazines that represent their students' wide range of interest. In Figures 3.1, 3.2, and 3.3, Lapp, Fisher, Flood, Goss-Moore, and Moore (2002) suggest guidelines by which to evaluate and select magazines, videos, and computer software.

How Should I Organize Learning Centers?

Learning centers are another way of accommodating the needs of second-grade students. Learning centers are designated areas of the classroom outfitted for students to perform meaningful tasks with specific objectives. In our interactions in elementary classrooms, we have found that many areas designated as learning centers are sometimes work areas where students engage in decontextualized activities—activities not directly related to what has been taught. Alternatively, we sometimes observe children engaged in activities that keep them busy but do not necessarily advance their ability to read and write. In both of these cases we are concerned that such learning center activities squander, rather than maximize, children's opportunities to learn. We are not alone in our concern. Ford and Opitz (2002) have noted that the way in which instruction is organized in many classrooms results in students actually spending less time with their teachers, and they ask how teachers can ensure that "the time away from the teacher [is] as powerful as the times spent with the teacher?" (p. 711). We believe that the answer to this question can be stated simply: An essential criterion of a learning center task is that its completion can be predicted to advance children's reading or writing performance. To meet that essential criterion, learning centers tasks must

Magazine Title _____

	Scale (1 = weak; 5 = excellent)				
1. Is current information provided?	1	2	3	4	5
2. Is a wide range of interest areas covered?	1	2	3	4	5
3. Is there a range of difficulty within a periodical?	1	2	3	4	5
4. Do the graphics support the text?	1	2	3	4	5
5. Are various types of graphics included (e.g., photographs, drawings, illustrations, cartoons)?	1	2	3	4	5
6. Is there a range of genres (e.g., stories, poems, essays, cartoons, experiments, puzzles)?	1	2	3	4	5
7. Are students invited to submit their writing, poetry, art?	1	2	3	4	5
8. Does the content support the curriculum goals?	1	2	3	4	5
9. Are instructional suggestions offered to the teacher?	1	2	3	4	5
10. Will the content motivate students to read?	1	2	3	4	5
	TOTAL:				

FIGURE 3.1. Guidelines for evaluating and selecting magazines.

From Lapp, Fisher, Flood, Goss-Moore, and Moore (2002). Copyright 2002 by Teachers College, Columbia University. Reprinted by permission. All rights reserved.

1. *Be evidence-based.* Credible research must indicate that the tasks being assigned will contribute to the children's development as capable readers and writers.

2. *Be accessible to students.* Assigned tasks must require use of skills and strategies that have been taught and that students are capable of applying independently. The purpose of the learning center activity is to engage students in sustained practice of what has been taught, thereby facilitating independence in reading or writing.

3. *Be connected* in some way to other literacy or content-area studies of the day or week.

Lesley M. Morrow (1989) recommends that learning centers be created as designated spaces that are partially separated from each other by bookshelves or other

Title _____					
	Scale (1 = weak; 5 = excellent)				
1. Does the video support curricular goals?	1	2	3	4	5
2. Are there corresponding text materials?	1	2	3	4	5
3. Is there an instructor's manual?	1	2	3	4	5
4. Are the graphics appropriate for the target grade level?	1	2	3	4	5
5. Is the language grade level appropriate?	1	2	3	4	5
6. Does the publisher provide a viewer's guide?	1	2	3	4	5
7. Is the information in the video historically accurate?	1	2	3	4	5
8. Does the video display people in respectful ways?	1	2	3	4	5
9. Does the video encourage students to read more about the topic?	1	2	3	4	5
10. Is the video reasonably priced?	1	2	3	4	5
	TOTAL:				

FIGURE 3.2. Guidelines for evaluating and selecting videos.

From Lapp, Fisher, Flood, Goss-Moore, and Moore (2002). Copyright 2002 by Teachers College, Columbia University. Reprinted by permission. All rights reserved.

furniture. She also recommends that (1) centers include learning resources that support completion of the assigned tasks (bulletin boards, white boards, or easels); (2) assigned tasks include some form of self-evaluation that allows students to check their own understanding; (3) there is a specified place for the students to put completed work; and (4) teachers devise a system for students to record, and teachers to track, that the task has been completed.

We share Morrow's (2002) belief that cycling children center to center should be highly structured. That is, as a teacher works with one group of children, the other children in the classroom should be systematically assigned to a particular learning center. Learning center activities should be planned so that children will be able to complete them within the expected time period (usually around 15 minutes). At the completion of each time period, children should move on to the next assigned center. Although the number and types of learning centers vary from classroom to classroom, in a typical second-grade classroom a teacher may have four learning centers: One is designated for independent or partner reading, where children read or reread a focal text; a second is designated as an independent writing center whose tasks might include writing on a topic that the children began in an earlier writing workshop, or writing in response to a prompt provided by the teacher; a third center is designated as a word study center, and the tasks give students an opportunity to practice word-making activities that support reading and spelling; a fourth center is a comprehension and language center, where students have the opportunity to listen to books on tape, read across texts using electronic or other print resources, or engage in language play and language development through poetry reading, readers' theatre, or peer-led book talks. Finally, it is helpful

---

Title _____

                                                                    Scale (1 = weak; 5 = excellent)

 1. Does the topic match curriculum goals?   1   2   3   4   5

 2. Do the instructional strategies and content match our   1   2   3   4   5
    philosophy?

 3. Is the material interactive?   1   2   3   4   5

 4. Is instructional feedback provided?   1   2   3   4   5

 5. Is the material easy to navigate?   1   2   3   4   5

 6. Are the directions language and user friendly?   1   2   3   4   5

 7. Can the material be used independently by the student?   1   2   3   4   5

 8. Can the program be re-entered without starting over?   1   2   3   4   5

 9. Are the skills levels appropriate for the student   1   2   3   4   5
    population?

10. Is learning enhanced by the graphics?   1   2   3   4   5

11. Is there an evaluation component?   1   2   3   4   5

12. Is a class spreadsheet available?   1   2   3   4   5

13. Is there a way to ensure student privacy?   1   2   3   4   5

14. Are additional extension lesson plans or materials   1   2   3   4   5
    included?

15. Can technical support be easily secured?   1   2   3   4   5

                                                                    TOTAL:

FIGURE 3.3. Guidelines for evaluating and selecting computer software.

From Lapp, Fisher, Flood, Goss-Moore, and Moore (2002). Copyright 2002 by Teachers College, Columbia University. Reprinted by permission. All rights reserved.

Making words learning center.

to have a list of purposeful activities that students can do if they finish their learning center activity before time for the next activity.

CLASSROOM ROUTINES THAT OPTIMIZE CHILDREN'S LITERACY LEARNING OPPORTUNITIES

A second-grade reading program must provide children with many opportunities to receive instruction in reading and writing, to practice reading and writing, and to use reading and writing as part of daily social interactions. Classroom settings in which children excel in learning to read and write are characterized as places where children are highly engaged as readers and writers (Gambrell, 1996). Excellent second-grade teachers know that although early literacy classrooms need to be places where print is abundant, accessible, and meaningful, they also need to provide students with predictable routines that increase their exposure to print and promote sustained practice in literacy. In the next section we briefly describe routines that are effective in providing second-grade students with substantial practice in reading, writing, listening, and speaking.

Morning Meeting

Morning meeting (Kriete & Betchel, 2002) is a format for beginning the school day. The

Cooperative learning pair.

Things to do During Literacy Time

Read around the room wi... ...nter

Read from your book box

Read a book to a partner

Read a big book

Read a fairytale or folktale

Read an ABC book

Read a book at Listening Center

Read books our class has written

Read from your journal

Read from your writing folder

Read an information book

Read at the overhead projector

Read a book on the computer

Read a holiday b...

LISTENING CENTER

Lists of independent reading activities (with clothespins marking the target tasks each day) help students to use their time wisely after finishing learning center assignments.

purpose of a morning meeting is to build a community of caring learners, to practice language skills, and to encourage social skills. A morning meeting typically lasts about 30 minutes and often uses a format that includes greeting, sharing, group activity, and news and announcements. The morning meeting practice is especially important to literacy development because it provides authentic and meaningful opportunities for children to read, write, speak, and listen. During the morning meaning, students are engaged in rich language discussions as they converse with each other and have many opportunities to read and reread a variety of texts, including daily announcements, letters from teachers, parents, or peers, and class chants and poems. The morning meeting is usually held in a common area of the classroom and includes activities around the calendar and daily events.

Teacher Read-Alouds

Teacher read-alouds are an effective way to expose second graders to a wide variety of genres, authors, and topics and to cultivate their appetites for reading. Read-alouds are especially beneficial to students who have had few experiences with storybook reading prior to coming to school. When students are read to by teachers and other adults, they (1) hear fluent reading; (2) develop listening skills; (3) increase their exposure to new and interesting words and concepts; and (4) increase their background knowledge.

Although the concept seems simple and widely familiar, the following guidelines may improve the read-aloud strategies of even experienced teachers (Graves, Juel, & Graves, 2004; Temple, Martinez, Yokota, & Naylor, 2002):

➢ Read several times a day, especially if your students have not been read to a lot.

➢ Select high-quality books with strong plots, interesting uses of language, and significant themes.

➢ Select books from a wide variety of genres, including informational text and poetry.

➢ Select age-appropriate books that are simple and short.

➢ Position the students so that they can all see the illustrations.

➢ Keep the introduction short. Most of the time should be spent reading aloud and discussing the text. Build background knowledge and vocabulary as needed, and invite the students to make predictions based on the title and illustrations.

➢ Stop at different points to show pictures and invite and encourage response.

➢ Encourage students to interact with text by sharing experiences and chanting phrases, especially in predictable books that have repeated words and phrases or cumulative rhyme.

➢ Provide opportunities for students to discuss the story either in a whole-class setting or in small peer-led groups.

Shared Reading

Shared reading, or shared reading experience (Holdaway, 1979), is a context for reading and rereading literature that is engaging and age appropriate. Students gather together, usually in a common meeting area, to read big books (large versions of authentic literature) or poems and chants displayed on a large chart. Students might also engage in shared reading by using individual copies of texts.

Shared reading allows teachers to help all children gain access to the same grade-appropriate text, thereby making more difficult books accessible to all students in the classroom (Fielding & Roller, 1992). Typically, the teacher introduces the selection by engaging students in effective prereading behaviors. Students might be asked to make predictions, engage in a picture walk, and activate their prior knowledge. The teacher uses this time to model and provides guided practice in the behaviors in which good readers engage before, during, and after reading.

A key feature of shared reading is its repeated reading component. After introducing the text to students, the teacher may ask students to move to another part of the classroom to read and reread the text alone and in pairs. At the same time, the teacher may select some students to stay with her to reread and review the strategies taught with the whole class. Then all the students can participate in the same prompt for writing and discussion.

Choral Reading

When students engage in choral reading, they read text aloud together. Choral reading can be teacher-led during shared reading; student-led in a small group as part of a learning center activity; or done with a peer during buddy reading. Choral reading is an important practice because, like partner reading, it can enable children to read text that is too difficult for them to read on their own. As such, it increases students' exposure to text and may provide a less threatening oral reading environment. In addition, choral readings support the development of reading accuracy and fluency, especially when they are used as a form of repeated readings.

Choral reading selections can be long or short; the text can contain stories, poems or information. Poems are particularly beneficial because most poetry is, as Temple et al. (2002) note, "anchored in sound and . . . intended to be read and recited aloud" (p. 452). In classrooms we have visited, we have observed students engaging in choral reading as part of morning meeting, during shared reading, and as an assigned learning center activity.

Partner Reading

When students engage in partner reading (sometimes called "buddy reading"), they pair off and read aloud from the same book. They may alternate reading sentences, paragraphs, or pages. Partner reading is typically used to support students' development of word-reading accuracy and fluency. When compared to other forms of reading, it has two particular benefits. First, unlike rereading independently, partner reading allows children to assist each other when encountering difficult words. Second, unlike the traditional practice of "round robin" reading, partner reading provides the opportunity to read the entire text, as students learn to follow along when their partner is reading, so that they can assist with unknown words. Like other types of reading, partner reading can be followed by some form of oral or written response to the text.

Buddy reading.

Sustained Silent Reading

Sustained silent reading (SSR) is an opportunity for students to "not merely read but live inside a book" (Block, 1999, p. 102). During SSRI, children read self-selected books and are given large blocks of uninterrupted time to establish their own purposes for reading. SSR increases the students' exposure to print, and as such, can contribute to the development of vocabulary, concept, and language knowledge, and word-reading accuracy and fluency (Anderson et al., 1988).

For young children who are just developing the habit of sustained reading, it is often helpful to allocate a very brief time for this activity at the beginning of the school year, and gradually increase the time as children become capable of extended periods of independent reading. For example, Graves et al. (2004) suggest setting aside 5- to 10-minute periods of reading and increasing the amount of time gradually, depending on the teacher's observations of children's engagement.

It is also useful to have children participate in establishing classroom rules for SSR. For example, in one classroom we visited, the students devised these rules for participation:

1. Choose enough books to read the whole time.
2. Stay in your seats.
3. Be respectful: Don't disturb others.

Teachers and students often post signs outside the classroom doors, reminding others when SSR is occurring, with the words "Shhh . . . SSR . . . Please don't disturb."

There are a number of ways for teachers to schedule SSR into their school day. Some teachers choose to tack it on to the end of morning or afternoon activities, using it as a time for students to engage in quiet, reflective reading. Others choose to include it as one of the learning centers in the classroom, so that all the children engage in it, but they do so at different times in their center rotations. In some schools there is a buildingwide SSR time, during which all members of the school community stop and engage in sustained reading of a book of choice.

However you engage your students in SSR, the important point to remember is that providing this time increases your students' opportunities to practice reading, expands their opportunities to acquire new vocabulary, concepts, and language structures, and also helps to convey to them that reading can bring enjoyment as well as knowledge.

Readers' Theatre

In Chapter 2 we introduced Readers' Theatre as a beneficial strategy, noting that it provides a creative context in which students can become more fluent readers. It is also an effective way to help make more difficult books accessible to all students (Fielding & Roller, 1992). In Readers' Theatre (Martinez, Roser, & Strecker, 1998/

1999; Temple et al., 2002) children use a text as a script for practicing the reading of literature; the aim is for students to practice their scripts through rereadings until they can accomplish a "polished" reading performance.

Different from acting out a story, Readers' Theatre requires no costumes, props, or memorization. Students use prepared scripts derived from real stories. Teachers can prepare these scripts themselves or ask older students to help. As Readers' Theatre has gained in popularity, more and more websites have been devoted to the presentation of prepared scripts. Some of these websites are listed in Chapter 8.

Readers' Theatre has many benefits. Because students must repeatedly practice a script to "learn" their parts, they get many opportunities to practice reading in a meaningful context. In addition, because students are expected to use their voices to bring their characters to life, Readers' Theatre requires children to consider character traits, actions, and motives and to use that information to "tell" the story in their character's words. As such, the sort of practice they engage in supports not just word-reading accuracy and fluency but also expressiveness. Because the ways in which we express words is a measure of comprehension, Readers' Theatre also facilitates the acquisition of this skill.

After a great deal of experience, second graders are quite capable of turning their regular reading texts into scripts. In one second-grade classroom we worked with a teacher who used Readers' Theatre on a regular basis. At the end of the year, a group of students were reading *Charlotte's Web*. At the end of each chapter, they turned a section of the chapter that had the most dialogue into a script and enjoyed "showing off" to their peers by performing these brief parts of the story. We observed the students practicing the same lines over and over. When we asked why they practiced the lines so many times, they explained that they had to "get the voices of the characters *perfect*, like Mrs. Thomas [their teacher] does."

Literature Circles

As we explained in Chapter 2 providing learning contexts in which children have opportunities to work together to make sense of what they read is consistent with cognitive theory, which indicates that learning is a social process and that students advance in their learning when they have the opportunity to talk, share, and reflect together. We briefly noted that literature circles—postreading discussion groups in which students talk about the books they have read—provide one context for collaborative learning. Small groups of students can join together either as part of a learning center or during a specific time scheduled to allow all students to participate in peer-led book discussions. The primary purpose of literature circles is for students to talk about the books they have read and work together to deepen their understanding.

However, literature circles also play other important roles. When teachers are free to observe children during peer-led discussions, they can gather information about how their students interact with text and with each other (Paratore, Garnick & Lewis, 1997). For example, teachers might find answers to these questions:

How do the students build on the comments of others to extend their understanding?

How do they use events in the text to justify their point of view?

How do they relate events in the text to their own lives or to other texts they have read?

Teachers can also learn about students' social behaviors. For example, as they observe children, they might ask:

How do students get the floor when they have something to say?

How do they articulate their agreement or disagreement?

How engaged are students when they think they are working away from the teacher's watchful eye?

In the second-grade classrooms we have visited, we have observed teachers using literature circles in different ways. For example, sometimes children were placed in groups according to ability. The teacher-selected books for each group all related to the same topic, but the book assigned to each group were matched to the independent reading levels of the children in that group. The children read the books independently, and after reading, they convened in small groups to discuss them. Then the class convened as a whole, and all of the children discussed what they learned about the focal topic.

In another example children were assigned to interest-based groups. The children in each group read a book about the same topic, but the selected books were at different levels of ability to match children's independent reading levels. After reading, children convened to talk about the topic about which they had each read, and what they had learned from their different books. In yet another example the teacher conducted student-led literature circles each day following SSR. One or two students a day (the student leaders) shared what they were reading and invited questions and comments from their peers. In another classroom we observed something slightly different. Students sat at their tables of four for SSR. Immediately following SSR, the group members shared what they had read that day. Then the teacher chose one student from each group to share with the whole class.

We recommend that literature circles be conducted with as few rules as possible and with minimal intervention from the teacher, thus providing an authentic context in which to talk about books. Teachers should act as mediators and facilitators, modeling effective ways to talk about books by sharing what they think about the books they are all reading.

Guided Reading

Guided reading involves teacher-led instruction and practice in specific decoding and comprehension strategies. Students are grouped homogeneously for guided reading groups, and teachers select texts that match the instructional reading level of the focal group of students. This means that the teacher expects that, given some help from her, students will be able to read approximately 95% of the words accurately.

Instruction during guided reading groups may focus on both word study and comprehension, and the duration is short, typically not exceeding 15 or 20 minutes per group. Guided reading groups may be conducted in many different ways, but a common format is that described by Fountas and Pinnell (1996). In this format, the teacher introduces the topic or story to the students, elicits prior knowledge, and invites them to make predictions. After modeling or reviewing a reading strategy and focusing on new vocabulary, the teacher directs the students to read the text, or a portion of the text, silently. The teacher may stop at different points to ask students to display the strategy taught, make connections, or draw conclusions. At times, the teacher may ask individual students to read aloud as he or she circulates among students in the group, jotting down information about fluency, accuracy, and strategies for constructing meaning.

Guided reading groups allow students to interact with text that is relatively easy to read with help from the teacher. If the students have few problems with decoding, they can spend more of their time constructing meaning. As students practice with the texts, and their fluency and accuracy improves, the teacher introduces increasingly difficult texts.

Writing Workshop

The writing workshop is a format for teaching writing that emphasizes process-based instruction (Piazza, 2002). Guidelines for conducting a writing workshop vary but typically include the following components.

➢ *Sharing*: Exemplary writing is shared with and by students as models of good writing.

➢ *Mini-lesson*: This component uses a direct instruction model—demonstration, guided practice, and independent practice—to teach focused lessons in grammar, conventions, and literary elements.

➢ *Writing and conferencing*: Students are given large amounts of time to apply what they learned in the mini-lesson. Teachers also conduct writing conferences, and students may engage in peer conferences.

➢ *Student sharing*: Students read aloud what they are writing and invite feedback to assist in revising their work.

The writing workshop is an important activity not only because of the theoretically sound instruction in the phases of the writing process (Bromley, 1999; Calkins, 1994; Graves, 1994), but also because it facilitates authentic connections between reading and writing. Published texts are used as exemplars of good writing; children learn to use what they read and what they know to plan their writing; they learn to read and reread their texts to monitor their writing; and they learn to share their texts with others to support revision and eventual publication.

A CLASSROOM VISIT

We have had many opportunities to visit the classroom of Pat Arterberry, a highly effective teacher from New Bedford, Massachusetts. Pat teaches in a small urban school that is identified as "high poverty." There are 18 children in her second-grade classroom, representing at least seven different cultures, including Portuguese, Cape Verdian, Santa Domingan, Puerto Rican, African American, and European American. Although no child in her classroom is identified as an English-language learner, the home language for some of the children is other than English. Three of the children have been referred for special services and are in the process of receiving formal identification as students with special needs.

Pat's classroom is bright, airy, and well organized. As you enter, it seems to resemble a home more than a classroom. Warm wooden floors are made cozier with colorful rugs; oversized windows are draped with colorful curtains. Pat's classroom is very large, and she has designed many snug spots in which students can get lost in books. Comfortable pillows and cushions soften corners. The students' desks are arranged in clusters to encourage cooperation and conversation. An immediate impression is that this is a place where learning is student centered.

In one corner of the room is the classroom library and common meeting area, where the morning meeting and other large-group instructional events occur. Bookshelves contain hundreds of selections that represent a variety of genres and reading levels to accommodate all of her second graders. Many picture books and chapter books are shelved with the spines facing out. However, Pat also has additional displays of books in colorful bins and crates; in these inviting containers students can see the covers easily and make a selection from the many books that are categorized as fiction and nonfiction. Pat also has a large collection of *Pair-It* books (www.harcourtachieve.com, search for "pair-it"). These trade books pair narrative and expository books with similar topics and themes. A versatile easel—one that has a melamine board on one side and a ledge and containers for an easel pad and markers on the other—makes this area a perfect spot for children and the teacher to write together as well.

The writing center is a place where literacy is practiced through meaningful and purposeful writing. The center contains the materials needed for Pat's second graders to work independently, with minimum guidance from her. Students can work on assigned writing, experiment with self-selected writing, or use the space to revise, edit, and publish their own work. It is also a place where small groups of three or four students work collaboratively on writing projects.

The writing center is set aside with tables, chairs, and low shelving. It is also in close view of the word wall, which creates an interactive dynamic: The students use the word wall when writing, and the word wall grows as students are introduced to more and more high-frequency words. The writing center also contains a bulletin board and wall space to display student work. The materials contained in the center are organized in bins, labeled, and easily accessible to all students. Pat's writing centers allows students ample opportunities to go beyond what was learned and practiced in the writing workshop. Fulfilling the requirements of a good "writing spot" (Morrow, 1989, 2002), it contains the following materials:

1. Various types and sizes of paper.

2. Writing materials and implements such as small white boards, dry erase markers, chalk boards, chalk, pencils (all sizes and colors), drawing markers, and crayons.

3. Things with which to make books (scissors, glue, stapler, blank-shape books).

4. Word collections (in addition to the word wall) stored in file boxes or cans.

5. Books of various genres.

6. Dictionaries and thesauruses.

7. A message board.

8. Student-generated work.

9. Writing folders and work samples.

10. Poster of the second-grade writing standards.

11. Scoring rubrics for writing.

Another area holds a large rectangular table with six chairs and serves as the location for guided reading and other small-group instruction. Encircled by low shelves that hold the baskets of texts used by the students during guided reading, this area is also well-organized. Pat has also set aside this space as a quiet area; students may choose this area to read, write, and work on individual projects.

Three computers form the technology center, where Pat sets up software programs for the students to use during their learning center and guided reading time. The students are well trained to use the computers; they work in pairs to interact with software that is geared to give them sustained practice in reading.

Wall and white board space offer more opportunities for Pat and her students to display print in a meaningful way. On the white board at the front of the classroom, Pat posts "Our Daily Agenda," which changes daily. In addition, she exhibits "Strategies Good Readers Use." After Pat models a reading strategy and the students have been given guided practice, a student displays the strategy on a poster for future reference. Pat says that students refer to these strategies each day before they read. Additional wall space is used to display student work in different stages. Students' writing assignments, art work, and book projects are proudly showcased on bulletin boards.

We know Pat well and have seen her teach many times. During our last visit we observed Pat's classroom space with new eyes, asking ourselves: What conclusions would a newcomer draw about how Pat views her role as a teacher? We answered our own query in this way. We think that a newcomer would perceive that Pat's classroom belongs to her students and that her role is to teach her students to be skillful and collaborative, yet independent. She organizes her classroom in a way that helps students work cooperatively to find answers to their questions, explore their own curiosities, and solve their own problems. We think a newcomer would also see that Pat has paid attention to evidence about the characteristics of learning environments in which children are motivated and engaged in learning.

LOOKING BACKWARD AND FORWARD

In this chapter we presented ways in which excellent second-grade teachers create effective literacy learning environments. We examined issues related to the arrangement of physical space as well as the reading and writing routines that influence children's opportunities to learn. We also visited Pat Arterberry's classroom, a second-grade teacher who works in the type of school setting that many identify as challenging. From Pat we learned how a thoughtful and well-prepared teacher applies research-based evidence in ways that make a difference for the children each and every day.

In Chapter 4 we shift our attention from the contexts and strategies that characterize effective teaching to those that comprise effective assessment. Once again, we begin with a brief overview of related research evidence and then describe specific strategies for assessing critical literacy domains. We also take a look at portfolios as one way for teachers and children to work together to organize their evidence of the children's learning progress. We then travel to the island of Nantucket, where we visit Shauna DiLuca, a relatively new second-grade teacher who is learning to assess her students by using classroom-based literacy assessments.

Try It Out

1. Take a close look at your classroom library. Are your books attractively arranged in a variety of ways? Are they organized according to author, genre, topic, or theme? Do they represent a variety of genres: realistic fiction, historical fiction, fantasy, poetry, traditional literature (folktales, fairytales, tall tales), and information? Do you have both picture books and chapter books? Most important: Are there engaging and appealing books for all learners? Are there texts that excite the lowest-performing readers? Are there books that challenge the highest-performing readers? If you answer no to any of these questions, make a list of the types of books you need to add and check with your school librarian to see if there is a way to add these to you collection.

2. Reread the criteria for setting up effective learning centers. Plan two or three centers and then check your plans against the criteria. Do the tasks meet the criteria established in the chapter?

3. Collect poems and chants that are playful and engaging. Record them on chart paper to read and reread with your students. Use a variety of repeated readings: teacher read-aloud, echo reading, and choral reading. Make books of the poems for the students to use when buddy reading, silent reading, and family reading.

4. Use the references in Chapter 8 to find a website on Readers' Theatre. Check out the website and select a script to use with your children. Try it out and share your reflections with a teaching colleague.

CHAPTER 4

GETTING TO KNOW YOUR STUDENTS

I n the previous chapters we focused on evidence-based instruction of reading, and we paid attention to *what* to teach and *how* to teach it. But you will recall that, in Chapter 1, we made the claim that excellent teachers also discover what students *already know* about reading and writing so that they know *when* to teach particular skills and strategies. In this chapter we explore the assessments and assessment practices that excellent teachers use to get to know their students and make sound instructional decisions to meet their needs.

FUNDAMENTAL ASSESSMENT PRINCIPLES

In today's classrooms the emphasis on assessment and accountability is largely inescapable. In states throughout our nation, teachers and children are held accountable for performance on tests that are purported to measure children's achievement of designated standards. These tests can be important and useful: as large-scale assessments, they can point to trends in a school, a district, or a community. But such tests yield little reliable information about children's day-to-day progress and the central question of interest to most teachers: *Have my children learned what I have taught today?* The answer to this question is critical to lesson planning, for it helps us to know whether or not we are meeting children's learning needs as a matter of routine. But the task of discovering if children are making progress from day to day is especially challenging because there are no ready-made tests to pull out of a file. That is, to know whether or not children have learned what we have taught, we must learn to use what children do on a daily basis as evidence. In one sense, this sounds like an easy task—collect what children do, toss it into a folder, and *presto*—we have evidence of their daily progress. But, of course, such a folder would provide a very limited record of children's literacy knowledge. We would have a window into what the child had written down, but what about the literacies that can only be observed—abilities such as fluency and accuracy, or comprehension-monitoring behaviors such as rereading or finding information on a lookback, or comprehension and response evident during book talks or literature circles (Paratore, Garnick, & Lewis, 1997)?

What does an excellent teacher do to document and respond to the range of literacies children have and use? Developing a systematic and effective plan for assessment begins with an understanding of fundamental assessment principles. Winograd, Flores-Dueñas, and Arrington (2003) caution that "no particular assessment is a best practice in and of itself; rather, the quality of assessments lies largely in how wisely they are used" (p. 205). They suggest that effective practice is most likely to be realized when assessment occurs within a context in which "teachers and students can work side by side in a trusting relationship that focuses on growth, nurturance, and self-evaluation" (p. 206).

With this context in mind, Winograd et al. (2003) suggest the guidelines presented in Figure 4.1 for implementing best practices in literacy assessment. These principles may be fundamental to creating a framework for assessment, but what should guide the actual collection of information? How does an excellent teacher gather the evidence needed to make instructional decisions? In the next section we examine the day-to-day practices on which excellent teachers rely to operationalize these principles.

"TRIED-AND-TRUE" ASSESSMENT STRATEGIES

Numerous books have been written about classroom assessment, with virtually hundreds of ways identified by which to collect evidence of performance and participate in efficient record-keeping. Suggestions include surveys, interviews, observational checklists, self-reflection, and anecdotal records. For a seasoned teacher, the number of suggestions and options can be staggering; we can imagine how overwhelming it must be for a *new* second-grade teacher. Choosing a repertoire of strategies that is user-friendly, comprehensive, and multidimensional is difficult. For this reason we have chosen to highlight the practices that we, and the teachers with whom we work, have found to be "tried and true." The practices that made our tried-and-true list met three criteria: First, they addressed a significant literacy

- Focus on important goals and support meaningful student learning.
- Are based on our most current and complete understanding of literacy and children's development.
- Are based in the classroom rather than imposed from outside.
- Use criteria and standards that are public, so that students, teachers, parents, and others know what is expected.
- Start with what the students currently know.
- Involve teachers (and often students) in the design and use of the assessment.
- Empower teachers to trust their own professional judgments about learners.
- Nourish trust and cooperation between teachers and students.
- Focus on students' strengths rather than just reveal their weaknesses.
- Provide information that is used to advocate for students rather than to penalize them.
- Support meaningful standards based on the understanding that growth and excellence can take many forms.
- Are integral parts of instruction.
- Gather multiple measures over time and in a variety of meaningful contexts.
- Provide educators and others with richer and fairer information about all children, including those who come from linguistically and culturally diverse backgrounds.
- Are part of a systemic approach to improving education that includes strengthening the curriculum, professional development for teachers, and additional support for helping those children who need it.
- Provide information that is clear and useful to students, teachers, parents, and other stakeholders.
- Continually undergo review, revision, and improvement.

FIGURE 4.1. Best practices in literacy assessment . . .

From Winograd, Flores-Dueñas, and Arrington (2003, pp. 208–209). Copyright 2003 by The Guilford Press. Reprinted by permission.

ability—that is, finding out students' knowledge of the focal ability was considered to be consequential in planning instruction. Second, the practices were judged to be "efficient"—that is, they could be expected to yield considerable diagnostic information in a short period of time. Third, the practices were pragmatic—that is, each could be readily implemented in a typical classroom setting, over time, and in a variety of ways.

We have organized the strategies on our list into seven categories: attitudes, interests, and motivation; metacognitive awareness; vocabulary and concept knowledge; phonemic awareness, fluency, accuracy, and word identification strategies; comprehension; and writing. In the section that follows, we describe each type of assessment and offer guidelines for implementation. As you will learn as we explore the various assessment strategies, some practices are expected to be ongoing, occurring daily or weekly within the context of routine instruction. Other assessments are likely to be administered only a few times a year. One point to remember is that the decisions you make about how or when to assess a child or a group of children should not be driven by any form of predetermined schedule but by a thoughtful response to the needs you observe as you watch and listen to your children, day in and day out.

Assessing Interest

The purpose of interest surveys is straightforward: They provide a way for students to tell you about their interests and attitudes toward reading and writing. This information is important because studies indicate that student engagement affects performance; interest is a factor that influences engagement (Guthrie & Wigfield, 2000). Knowing about students' interests can help you to plan instruction in various ways. For example, you might use information from surveys to help students choose books for independent reading, to choose books for reading aloud, or to generate topics for writing. The results might influence the ways in which you organize books in the classroom library. That is, you might deliberately organize according to topics in which students have expressed interest. Conversely, survey results can help you expand students' interests (Rhodes & Shanklin, 1993). By analyzing what your students *do not* mention, you can choose books for reading aloud that will increase their exposure to topics, authors, titles, and genres that are, as yet, unfamiliar to them. You can periodically showcase new topics and book titles in your classroom library, as a way of developing interest in preparation for a particular unit of study. In writing and technology centers, you can help your students explore unfamiliar topics through Web-based searches.

Surveys can take many different forms, but they are typically presented in two ways: One type of survey presents statements about student interests in reading and writing (e.g., "I like to read books at home." "I like to write at home."), and students rate themselves by indicating how strongly the statement represents their own feelings. A second format is more open-ended. The survey poses questions such as, "What kind of books do you like to read?" and "What kinds of things do you like to write about?" and the students respond by composing lists of ideas or a brief narrative.

Many published surveys are available; one example is presented in Figure 4.2. One benefit of published surveys is that they often have well thought out scoring guidelines that have been field tested. Alternatively, you might choose to develop your own survey. Caldwell (2002) states that designing your own student-generated survey is simple, and she provides the following useful guidelines:

➢ Ask children to tell you about their reading and writing interests. You can do this by asking them to brainstorm titles, authors, and topics during a whole-

---

Here's How I Feel about Reading

Name _____

1. I like to read about _____ .

2. My friends think reading is _____ .

3. My favorite book is _____ .

4. At home, reading is _____ .

5. On weekends, my favorite thing to do is _____ .

6. When I get older, I'll read _____ .

7. I like books about _____ .

8. When we read library books at school, I _____ .

9. The best thing about reading is _____ .

10. The worst thing about reading is _____ .

FIGURE 4.2. Attitude and interest inventory.

From McKenna and Stahl (2003, p. 212). Copyright 2003 by The Guilford Press. Reprinted by permission.

class discussion while you record their ideas, or have them page through their reading textbooks and indicate which topics and genres are of interest to them.

➢ Record all the information on a chalkboard or chart.

➢ On a sheet of paper, transfer the entire list or the top three or four choices of topics or genres and give one to each student.

➢ Ask students to indicate the topics that most interest them by circling or checking them.

By using this method, Caldwell explains, you will include only the key elements that elicit interest in your students.

Another way to assess children's reading interests is through the use of book logs in which students document what they read and how they feel about what they read. A book log helps students keep track of the books they read, determine the difficulty of those books, and reflect on their feelings about the books. Book logs can be followed by a self-assessment in which students reflect on the books they have read over several days and weeks and draw conclusions about their reading habits.

In our classroom visits we have seen many examples of book logs. They typically include space for students to write the title of books they have read and often a comment about the ease or difficulty of the text and their response to it. In some cases teachers follow up once a month with a self-assessment of the book logs. Questions include identifying their favorite books, making connections with characters, and identifying how they improved as readers. An example of a book log is included in Figure 4.3. Notice that at the bottom of the log, there is a prompt for the student to reflect on the collection of readings.

Assessing Metacognitive Awareness

In Chapter 2 we discussed the importance of students' awareness about the processes in which they engage during reading and writing. We explained that students who can describe and explain the thought processes they use as they read and write are often better able to control and regulate those processes. For example, readers who are metacognitively aware notice when their reading is not making sense, and they initiate a strategy to "fix up" the misunderstanding. The importance of metacognitive awareness in successful independent reading makes it an extremely pertinent area of knowledge to assess. One way to assess this knowledge is through metacognitive awareness interviews. These interviews examine students' thought processes as they learn to become competent readers and writers. The purpose of these interviews is for the teacher to learn what goes on inside the minds of his or her students as they try to read, write, and work to understand text. Also called process interviews (Paratore & Indrisano, 1987), metacognitive awareness interviews can be held informally during ongoing reading and writing activities, or they can be scheduled, structured events.

Interviews differ from surveys in two important ways. First, because interviews are oral rather than written interactions, they are conducted with individuals (or, in some cases, with a small group of students) rather than with the whole class. Second, in the best cases, they resemble conversations between the teacher and student. As such, the particular questions asked may change based on the "flow" of the conversation. That is, although the teacher usually has a list of the questions she intends to ask, students' responses may take her in a different direction and prompt her to ask different questions.

Metacognitive awareness interviews usually begin with questions that are intended to prompt students to articulate their perceptions about reading and writing. A list of questions drawn from the work of Majorie Lipson and Karen Wixson (2003) is shown in Figure 4.4.

Johnston (1997) suggests that teachers ask questions using terms that invite

Name _____ _____ Month _____

What Did I Read?				What Do I Think?
Date Started	Book Title and Author	Date Finished	Easy, Hard, or Just Right?	

Look at all the books you read this month. Which one did you like best?

On the back of this paper tell what it is and why you liked it.

FIGURE 4.3. Book log.

From *Teaching Literacy in Second Grade* by Jeanne R. Paratore and Rachel L. McCormack. Copyright 2005 by The Guilford Press. Permission to photocopy this figure is granted to purchasers of this book for personal use only (see copyright page for details).

Student Interview

Questions designed to elicit students' awareness of various aspects of the reading and writing process might include:

Functions, goals and purposes of reading and writing

- What is reading (or writing)?
- What are some of the reasons people write (read)?
- Why do people read (or write)?

Self-appraisal and goal setting

- Describe yourself as a reader (writer).
- Tell me two things you can do now in writing (reading) that you didn't used to be able to do.
- What would you like to do better as a reader (writer)?
- What is there about writing (reading) that you still don't understand?
- What kind of help do you think you need with reading? In writing?
- How long do you think it will take for you to read as well as you want or need to read?
- Who is the best writer (reader) you know?
- What does that person do that makes her/him such a good writer (reader)?
- How could you improve your reading (writing)?

Knowledge about reading/writing skills and strategies

- Do you read in a different way when you're reading different kinds of things?
- Are some things easier to write about than others?
- How do you decide what to read (write)?
- What do you do when you have trouble during reading and writing?
- How do you get started in writing?

Attitudes and motivation

- Do you write (read)? What?
- What are some titles of books that you've enjoyed?
- What topics do you enjoy writing about?
- Have you ever had a teacher who made reading/writing fun and exciting? Tell me about her/him?
- Have you ever learned something just by writing (reading) about it?
- Have you had some experiences that have made you want to read (write) about something?
- Do your parents (or someone else) read to you? How often?
- Do you have a library card? Books? Magazines?

FIGURE 4.4. Metacognitive awareness interview.

From Lipson and Wixson (2003, p. 95). Published by Allyn and Bacon. Copyright 2003 by Pearson Education, Inc. Reprinted by permission.

the student to ponder a situation, such as asking a second grader "What would you do if a first grader asked you how to read?" In that way, teachers let the students do most of the talking. Johnston cautions teachers to avoid interrupting and dominating the conversation, and reminds teachers that, "The more you listen, the more you will learn" (p. 181). In addition, Johnston provides the following useful guidelines for conducting interviews:

➢ Establish a legitimate need for the information. Let the students know that the information they give you will be useful to you as you teach them to read and write.

➢ Check on student understanding and facilitate student talk by saying things like, "That sounds interesting. Tell me more."

➢ Don't ask questions to which you already know the answer or ones that have a right or wrong answer.

➢ Make it concrete. If a child says, "When I come to a word I don't know, I sound it out," ask him [or her] for an example.

➢ Use the student's own terminology. This shows that you are trying to make sense of what the student says and reduces the likelihood that you will be putting words in the student's mouth.

➢ Encourage reflectiveness. This can reduce your role as the evaluator and show the student that you are a partner in the process.

➢ After recording the student's responses, analyze them. Ask yourself: What does the student know? What does the student almost know? What does the student still need to learn?

Students' responses to interview questions should help you to focus your instruction. For example, if you find that some or most of your students are unable to answer, even with additional probing, the question, "What do you do to help yourself remember what you read?", you might decide that you need to be more explicit in your instruction of comprehension monitoring strategies. Or, if you discover that many of your students say only "I sound it out" when asked what they do when they come to a word they do not know, perhaps instruction in additional strategies for decoding unknown words is in order.

The metacognitive awareness interview can help you to understand what the students know and still need to know about the processes of reading and understanding text, and it can help you plan subsequent instruction. However, Rhodes and Shanklin (1993) remind us that metacognitive awareness interviews also have

some potential problems. For example, in an effort to please the teacher, students may say what they think the teacher wants to hear, but they may not actually engage in the process. A student may say, "I always make a plan before I write," but the teacher may observe that the student rarely plans or organizes his or her writing beforehand, unless given a directive to do so.

Conversely, students may underestimate their own performance. That is, they may actually do more than they say, especially good readers whose reading strategies are so automatic that they have largely internalized the processes. As a consequence, they are not consciously aware of the strategies they use. For example, you might observe a student during sustained silent reading who always looks at a book's front and back cover and does a "picture walk" before reading. However, when asked what he or she does before reading, the student may answer that he or she looks at the title and then begins reading. These examples underscore the need to pay attention to Winograd et al.'s (2003) guideline that teachers use "multiple assessments over time in a variety of meaningful contexts" (p. 209) to construct an understanding of students' literacy strengths and needs. In this example, the multiple sources would include the interview and observations of students as they read and write in the classroom.

Another potential problem highlighted by Rhodes and Shanklin is that some questions may be misinterpreted by students, especially if the language or terminology is unfamiliar. Teachers can minimize the occurrence of problems of this type by using child-friendly language and using follow-up questions.

Excellent teachers are alert to these potential drawbacks, and they take steps to maximize the trustworthiness of the information they gather. In addition, as with every other assessment practice, they consider interviews as only one source of evidence about students' understanding of reading and writing, and they consider what children *say* along with what they observe children *doing*.

Assessing Phonemic Awareness

Recall that in Chapter 2 we described phonemic awareness as the ability to distinguish individual sounds in words. Research suggests that phonemic awareness is a strong predictor of reading success, and further, that when children receive explicit instruction that improves their awareness of phonemes, they experience greater success in learning to read (National Reading Panel, 2000).

Assessing phonemic awareness can be done easily with a quick test called the Yopp–Singer Test of Phoneme Segmentation (Yopp, 1995). A copy of the test is included in Figure 4.5. Administering this test takes approximately 5–10 minutes, and the directions are straightforward. It is an oral test in which you ask the stu-

Student's name _____ Date _____

Score (number correct) _____

Directions: Today we're going to play a word game. I'm going to say a word and I want you to break the word apart. You are going to tell me each sound in the word in order. For example, if I say *old,* you should say "/o/-/l/-/d/."

(Administrator: Be sure to say the sounds, not the letters, in the word.) Let's try a few together.

Practice items: Assist the child in segmenting these items as necessary: *ride, go, man.*

Test items: Circle those items that the student correctly segments; incorrect responses may be recorded on the blank line following the item.

1. dog _____   12. lay _____

2. keep _____   13. race _____

3. fine _____   14. zoo _____

4. no _____   15. three _____

5. she _____   16. job _____

6. wave _____   17. in _____

7. grew _____   18. ice _____

8. that _____   19. at _____

9. red _____   20. top _____

10. me _____   21. by _____

11. sat _____   22. do _____

FIGURE 4.5. Yopp–Singer Test of Phonemic Segmentation.

From Yopp (1995). Copyright 1995 by the International Reading Association. Reprinted by permission.

dent to break apart 22 one-syllable words into individual phonemes. On the record sheet, document what the student says and calculate the score according to the percentage of correct answers.

Assessing Fluency, Accuracy, and Word Identification Strategies

Assessing word knowledge requires that teachers document children's word-reading accuracy and fluency and determine what types of word identification strate-

ANSWER KEY

Student's name _____   Date: _____

Score (number correct) _____

Directions: Today we're going to play a word game I'm going to say a word and I want you to break the word apart. You are going to tell me each sound in the word in order. For example, if I say *old*, you should say "/o/-/l/-/d/."

(Administrator: Be sure to say the sounds, not the letters, in the word.) Let's try a few together.

Practice items: Assist the child in segmenting these items as necessary: *ride, go, man.*

Test items: Circle those items that the student correctly segments, incorrect responses may be recorded on the blank line following the item.

1. dog /d/-/o/-/g/
2. keep /k/-/e/-/p/
3. fine /f/-/i/-/n/
4. no /n/-/o/
5. she /sh/-/e/
6. wave /w/-/a/-/v/
7. grew /g/-/r/-/oo/
8. that /th/-/a/-/t/
9. red /r/-/e/-/d/
10. me /m/-/e/
11. sat /s/-/a/-/t/
12. lay /l/-/a/
13. race /r/-/a/-/s/
14. zoo /z/-/oo/
15. three /th/-/r/-/e/
16. job /j/-/o/-/b/
17. in /i/-/n/
18. ice /i/-/s/
19. at /a/-/t/
20. top /t/-/o/-/p/
21. by /b/-/i/
22. do /d/-/oo/

FIGURE 4.5. *cont.*

gies children attempt when they encounter unknown words. In addition, assessing word knowledge requires that teachers assess children's vocabulary and concept knowledge and spelling abilities.

Running Records

In most second-grade classrooms, teachers listen to children read orally on a daily basis. Learning how to document these routine oral renderings of text is an important teaching skill. Johnston and Clay (1997) explain that "keeping a graphic record" (p. 193) helps the teacher (1) obtain instructionally relevant information at a glance; (2) provides useful data that allows the teacher to compare earlier and later performances of oral reading behaviors; and (3) aids record keeping in documenting the changes and planning instruction. By listening to students read aloud and recording their pattern of errors or "miscues" (Goodman, 1965), the teacher is able to make good decisions about what her students need to learn to become accurate readers. Recording oral reading can also help the teacher (1) group students with similar learning needs; (2) gauge the difficulty of classroom texts; and (3) provide information to share with students, parents, and other teachers (Cooper & Kiger, 2005).

Perhaps the most well known and widely used procedure for documenting children's oral reading behaviors is the running record (Clay, 2005). Running records are easy to administer and enable teachers to assess students at any time and with any text. McKenna and Stahl (2003; pp. 56–58) provided a summary of the guidelines:

> ➤ Inform the student that you will be listening to him or her read, and that you will be writing down some notes.

> ➤ Listen to a student read. Ideally, the text should be unfamiliar and between 100 and 200 words. Use authentic texts: "little books" with complete stories or informational texts.

Teacher administering a running record.

> As the child is reading, record the student's behaviors using a code on a blank sheet of lined paper, blank paper, or special record sheet provided in Clay's books.

> In addition to recording the errors the student makes, record attitudes, expression, finger pointing, intonation, word-by-word reading, and student's vocalizations and comments.

McKenna and Stahl also provide the instructions for the coding:

1. Mark every word read correctly with a check. Make lines of checks correspond to lines of text. Clay (1979) uses a solid line to indicate page breaks.

2. Record an incorrect response with a text under it. Each substitution is scored as an error.

3. Record an omission with a dash over the omitted word. Each omission is scored as an error.

4. Record insertions by writing the word on top and putting a dash beneath. Each insertion is scored as an error.

5. A self-correction occurs when a child has made an error and then corrects it. A self-correction is recorded by using the letters *SC* and is *not* considered an error.

6. A repetition is recorded with a line above the repeated segment of the text but is *not* scored as an error.

7. If a child hesitates for longer than 5 seconds because he or she has made an error, and does not now how to correct it, or if a child stops and makes no attempts, he or she is told the word. This pause is coded with a *T* (for *told*) on the bottom and scored as an error.

8. If a child asks (A) for help, the teacher responds, "Try something" and waits 3–5 seconds for an attempt before telling the child the correct word. This strategy enables the teacher to observe what problem solving strategies the child is likely to use when facing challenges in the text.

9. Sometimes a child loses his or her place or goes off on a tangent that is far removed from the text. In such a case, the teacher should say, Try that again" (TTA), and indicate the line, paragraph, or page where the child should restart. Record by putting brackets around the faulty section of reading and code *TTA* . The entire section is only coded as one error.

10. Other behaviors may be noted but not scored. Pausing, sounding out parts of the word, finger pointing, and unusually fast or slow reading rates and word-by-word reading should be noted on the running record and considered in the analysis but not included in quantitative scoring.

Figure 4.6 presents a summary of the coding symbols typically used in recording oral reading behaviors (see Johnston, 1997, p. 194). A sample of a running record is included in Figure 4.7.

Running records are scored for accuracy and self-correction rate. The accuracy rate is the percentage of words read correctly. The self-correction rate is the ratio of

What Is Said	During Reading	After Reading
Correct response	✓	✓
Omission	—	—
		text word
Substitution	spoken word	spoken word
		text word
Insertion	spoken word	spoken word
		—
Repetition	R	R
Attempt	attempt/attempt	attempt/attempt
		text word
Appeal for help	APP	attempt/APP
		text word
Teacher prompt: Tells the word	———————— /T	———————/——— text word / T
Asks to try again	/TA	/TA

FIGURE 4.6. Symbols for recording oral reading miscues.

Adapted from Johnston (1997, p. 194). Copyright 1997 by Stenhouse Publishers. Adapted by permission.

self-corrections to the total number of self-corrections plus errors. According to Marie Clay (2000), a selection is considered easy, or at the child's independent reading level, if the child obtains a score of 95–100%; it is at the child's instructional level if the accuracy score is within 90–94%; and too difficult (frustration level) if the score is below 90%.

McKenna and Stahl (2003, pp. 59–60) suggest a series of questions to guide teachers as they review and analyze students' miscues:

> *Meaning* (M): Did the reader choose a substitution or phrasing that makes sense in the passage or sentence or part of the sentence?

> *Structure cues* (S): Did the reading sound like language that follows a grammatical form? Did the reader follow the structure of the text?

> *Visual* (V): Did the child read a word that had graphic similarity to the word in the text? Was the graphophonic system being used?

> *Self-correction column*: What cueing system did the reader use to *fix* the errors?

Jake 10/4 Bony-Legs   96 Words
P 6–9

Page	Accuracy = 92.6% SC rate = 1:4	E	SC	Information used — E MSV	SC MSV
6	✓✓✓✓ =horrible ✓✓	I		(m)sv	
	✓✓✓				
	✓✓ i-i-✓ / iron				
	✓✓ lived / liked	I		ms(v)	
	✓✓✓✓				
	✓✓✓				
	✓✓✓✓				
	✓✓ stayed / stood ✓✓✓	I		ms(v)	
7	✓✓✓ ✓✓✓				
	was ✓✓✓✓	I		(m)sv	
	who ✓✓✓ grandmother/sc aunt	I	I	(m)sv	(m)sv
	✓✓R✓				
	said/sc ✓✓ sent		I		ms(v)
	✓✓ ✓✓✓				
8	✓✓ ✓✓✓ bu-bu/✓ butter				
	✓✓ bite / bit	I		(m)(s)(v)	
	✓✓				
	✓✓✓✓				
9	✓✓✓✓✓				
	✓✓ supper /APD surprised	I		ms(v)	
	✓✓✓				
	✓✓✓✓✓				
	✓✓✓				

FIGURE 4.7. Sample running record.

Once you take a close look at the patterns of errors made by students, you can learn a great deal about how each student reads words. Does the student use meaning when he or she reads? Is the student simply sounding out words? Does the student use what he or she knows about spoken language or the language of the text to make attempts at unknown words? Learning about the behaviors your students use when reading words makes instructional planning more focused.

Learning to take reliable running records takes practice. We advise you to (1) access the learning resources listed in Chapter 8, (2) take every opportunity to practice and refine your assessment skills, and (3) remember to consider the evidence you gather from running records along with all of the other sources of data that you are gathering.

Anecdotal Records and Observational Checklists

Another way to collect data about your students' decoding behaviors is through the use of anecdotal records and observational checklists. Anecdotal records are written comments based on observations; checklists are prepared sheets listing the behaviors you hope to observe. Both have many advantages (Rhodes & Shanklin, 1993). First, they are open-ended; you can observe anything you perceive to be significant. Second, they are unobtrusive; you can observe students while they are reading and interacting with text without interrupting them. Third, they are valid; you are assessing the behaviors students use as they complete routine reading and writing tasks.

Anecdotal observations are descriptive and include detail. You can record the events as they are happening, and the details can give you rich data about the process your students go through as they interact with text. Typically, teachers who rely on anecdotal records as one source of data carry a clipboard with sticky notes. As they sit with individuals or groups of students, they record on the sticky notes the behaviors they observe. Later, they transfer these comments onto individual student sheets and often include elaboration with each entry. These entries are meant to be reviewed at a later date by taking a look at the descriptions and examining patterns of behaviors. This information can help teachers plan subsequent instruction to meet individual needs.

Checklists can provide the same information but have the disadvantage of being static: They limit you to observing the behaviors that are listed on the page. For this reason you may need to add items and categories on the checklist as the year progresses.

An important advantage of using anecdotal records and observational checklists is their versatility. They can be used in a variety of settings and for a variety of reasons. You can observe your students as they read independently or with a partner, as they interact in discussions, cooperatives group activities, or as they work in learning centers.

Assessing Vocabulary and Concept Knowledge

Assessing vocabulary is a complex task. Children learn between 1,000 and 3,000 new words each year (Nagy, 1986), and the number and kinds of words vary among students. Word knowledge is dependent on the students' background knowledge, the amount of reading in which they engage, and the instruction they have received.

Camille Blachowicz and Peter Fisher (2002) have devised several authentic ways to assess students' word and concept knowledge. In planning for vocabulary assessment, they suggest that teachers: assess (1) breadth, to learn how broad a range of words students know; (2) usage, to learn about students' ability to use words "flexibly and richly" (p. 140); and (3) acquisition of the particular words taught. We have chosen one method from each category to illustrate different ways in which effective teachers can assess their students' vocabulary knowledge. We especially like these because they begin with what students already know.

Assessing Vocabulary Breadth before Reading

Before reading, especially in content areas such as math, science, and social studies, it may be useful for teachers to ask their students what they already know about the words they will be learning and using. For example, in Figure 4.8, the teacher gives students a list of words that they will be studying during a unit on space. The students are asked to look at each word and rate their knowledge according to the following criteria: (1) I can use it! (2) I've heard of it! (3) I don't know!

The students place a checkmark in the box that applies to each word. Then they work together to discuss the words on the page. Teachers review the information and ask themselves questions such as (in this example): How many students can use the word star? How many students have heard of the word galaxy? Using the chart and the answers to the follow-up questions, teachers then plan instruction and place particular emphasis on the words for which the students demonstrated the least amount of knowledge. The same chart can be used by the students after the unit of study and then compared with the original assessment. The benefit of this assessment is that students have an opportunity to think about word meanings before they begin to read, then work with each other to negotiate meaning, then assess their understanding at the end of the unit.

Assessing Usage: Three-Minute Meetings

Three-minute meetings can be used to assess how well students can use words from a word wall, word bank, or individual word list related to a particular theme

Word	I can use it!	I've heard of it!	I don't know!
star	✓		
Milky Way		✓	
planet	✓		
Earth		✓	
satellite		✓	
galaxy			✓
Big Dipper		✓	
space	✓		
moon	✓		
universe		✓	

FIGURE 4.8. Before reading knowledge rating.

Adapted from Blachowicz and Fisher (2002, p. 139). Copyright 2002 by Pearson Education, Inc. Upper Saddle River, NJ. Adapted by permission.

or topic. In a 3-minute meeting a teacher selects several words from a collection and meets with each student individually to discuss the words. The students can either talk about the words, show how they used the words in their writing, or a combination of both. The teacher notes how well students used the word in a meaningful way. Blachowicz and Fisher (2000) recommend conducting a few such meetings each day over a 1- to 2-week period. In addition, they suggest that students become involved in the selection of words to be used in the meetings. They can work in groups to devise the word lists and even conduct some 3-minute meetings with each other.

Assessing Particular Words

Blachowicz and Fisher (2002) agree that teachers sometimes need quick teacher-made assessments that evaluate their students' ability to make associations between words. They suggest designing recall-type tests that require the students to define words by the following criteria:

1. Giving/choosing a synonym (*sunset* is *dusk*).
2. Giving/choosing a classification (*Earth* is a *planet*).
3. Giving/choosing examples (the *Big Dipper* is a *constellation*).

4. Giving/choosing an explanation of how something is used (a *telescope* is an *instrument used to view the sky*).

5. Giving/choosing an opposite (*east* is opposite from *west*).

6. Giving/choosing a definition (the *sun* is *the nearest star to Earth*).

7. Giving/choosing a picture.

An effective was to assess young children's understanding of word meanings is through illustration. Figures 4.9 and 4.10 present one second-grade child's illustration of his understanding of the concepts of *fire* and *ice*, and the concepts of *fight* and *dual*. In Figure 4.11, the teacher assessed a child's knowledge of a concept taught in science, levers, through written explanation.

Assessing Comprehension

Comprehension is a broad construct, and there are many ways to assess it. Here we focus on just two: oral retellings and anecdotal records and observational checklists.

Retelling of Narrative Text

Oral retelling provides information about comprehension as a process and a product (Rhodes & Shanklin, 1993). It allows teachers to assess what students remem-

FIGURE 4.9. Student work sample: Synonyms.

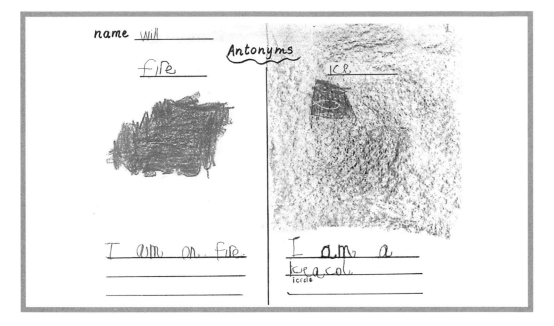

FIGURE 4.10. Student work sample: Antonyms.

ber about what they read without direct questioning or support from a teacher. Story retelling can reveal students' sense of story: Retelling of expository text can reveal students' understanding of main ideas and details. Retelling of narrative text is the most common form of retelling. Morrow (2002) states that story retelling allows students to make inferences and draw conclusions by organizing and integrating information that is not explicitly stated. When retelling, students need to synthesize information, make connections to their own lives and experiences, and paraphrase events and story elements in sequential order.

Story retelling is conducted one on one with teacher and student, and it can be individualized by matching an appropriate text with each student. Rhodes and Shanklin (1993) suggest using the following procedure:

1. Select a text to read (the text should have a clear plot).
2. Let the student know that you will be asking him or her to retell after he or she reads.
3. Have the student read the text silently.
4. After the student has finished reading the text, ask him or her to put the text aside and retell everything he or she can remember.

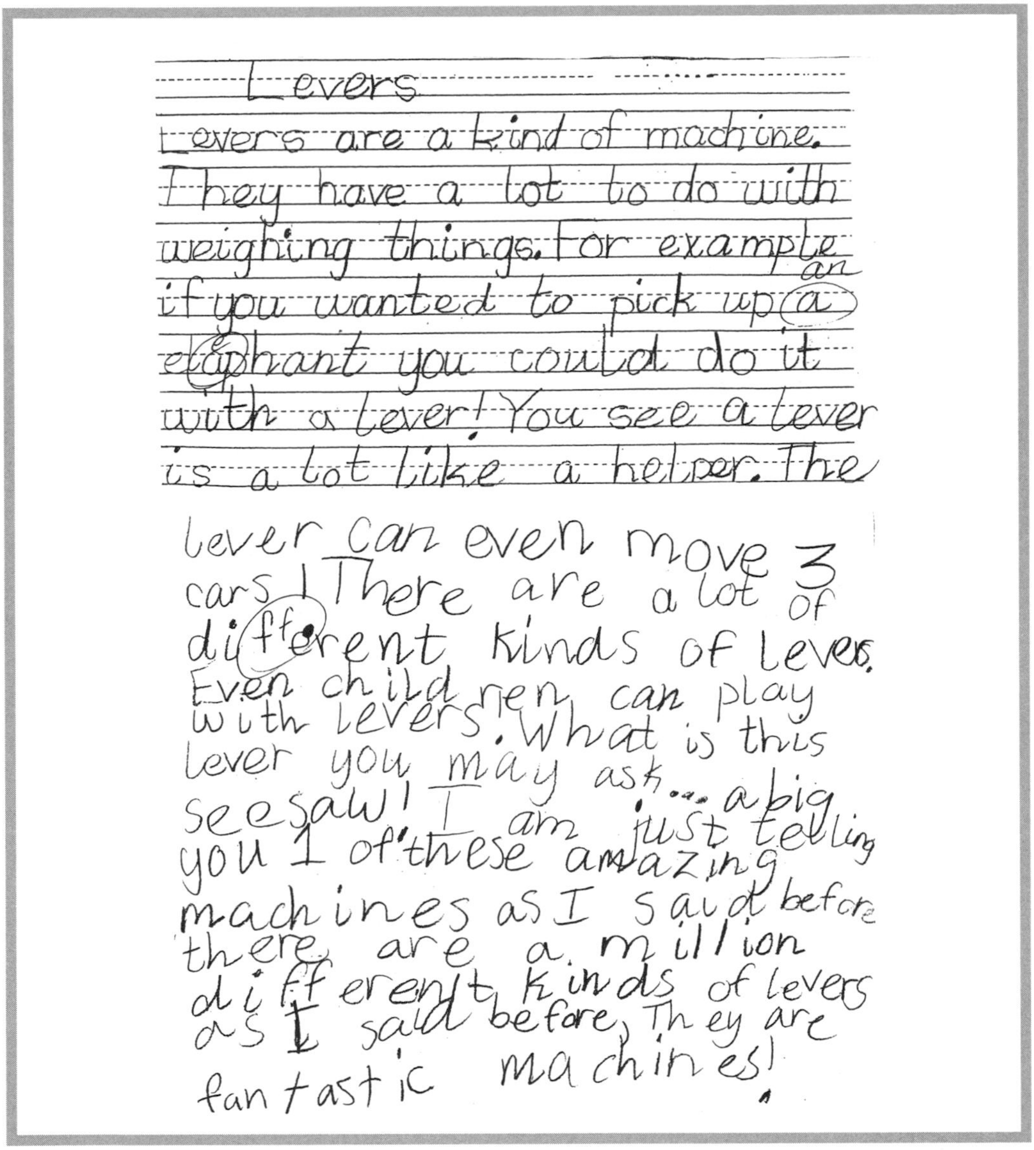

Levers

Levers are a kind of machine. They have a lot to do with weighing things. For example, if you wanted to pick up an elephant you could do it with a lever! You see a lever is a lot like a helper. The lever can even move 3 cars! There are a lot of different kinds of Levers. Even children can play with levers. What is this lever you may ask... a big seesaw! I am just telling you 1 of these amazing machines as I said before there are a million different kinds of levers as I said before. They are fantastic machines!

FIGURE 4.11. Student work sample: Levers.

5. When finished, ask the student if there is anything else he or she would like to add to the retelling.

6. Follow up with questions, if necessary.

7. Analyze the retelling.

Morrow (2002) suggests parsing, or dividing, a story into story elements ahead of time and using the parsed text as a list for checking comprehension—setting, problem/goal, plot episodes, resolution, and consequence—then checking off the student's inclusion of story elements and noting if the retelling is sequential. When analyzing the retelling, Caldwell (2002) offers the following questions:

Did the retelling focus on the important elements of character, setting, problem, events, and resolution?

Was the retelling sequential?

Was the retelling accurate?

Did the retelling include inferences?

Did the students offer personal reactions?

In Figure 4.12 we present a retelling checklist developed by Joy Turpie and Mary Matthews and published in a position paper of the Massachusetts Reading Association (Paratore et al., 1992). Notice that this checklist assumes a dynamic assessment stance. That is, if the student has difficulty recalling important parts of the story, the teacher may engage him or her in a number of intervention strategies to determine the condition or circumstance that enables the student to be successful.

We offer one caution about story retellings as an assessment procedure. Johnston (1997) reminds us that story retelling is not an authentic activity. As he points out, in real life, we would not ask someone to retell something we had read or seen. In fact, many children are confused when adults ask them to retell something they have read themselves. Additionally, some students are naturally more able to retell stories because they have more exposure to stories and story structure. Johnston reminds us that if story retellings have not been a part of their instruction, many students may do poorly not because they do not understand the story but because they do not understand the assessment task. As in the use of any assessment, it is important to consider the extent to which the task is a good match for the instruction.

Retelling of Expository Text

The same retelling procedures can be used to assess comprehension of expository or informational text. After students read a selection from an expository text, ask them to retell what they think is important while you record their responses on a blank sheet of paper and identify the important parts mentioned by the student. In the case of expository text, we expect students to be sensitive to the nonfiction text structure. For example, if the overarching text structure is problem–solution, the students may arrange their retelling according to a problem-solution organiza-

	Interventions				
	Initial Retelling	Prompt	Structured Prompt	Visual Walk-Through	Rereading	Comments
1. SETTING						
a. Names main character(s).	——	——	——	——	——	——
b. Names other characters.	——	——	——	——	——	——
c. Includes statement about time and place.	——	——	——	——	——	——
2. PROBLEM/GOAL						
Refers to main character's primary toal or problem to be solved.	——	——	——	——	——	——
3. WAYS TO SOLVE THE PROBLEM						
Relates an event or series of events that lead the main character toward solving the problem or reaching the goal.	——	——	——	——	——	——
4. RESOLUTION						
a. Names a problem solution/goal attainment.	——	——	——	——	——	——
b. Ends retelling with a concluding statement.	——	——	——	——	——	——
5. SEQUENCE						
Retells story in structural order (setting, problem/goal, ways to solve the problem, resolution).	——	——	——	——	——	——

Name: _____ Date: _____
Title of story: _____
Examiner: _____

FIGURE 4.12. Assessing story retelling.

From *Teaching Literacy in Second Grade* by Jeanne R. Paratore and Rachel L. McCormack. Copyright 2005 by The Guilford Press. Permission to photocopy this figure is granted to purchasers of this book for personal use only (see copyright page for details).

tion—or, as the case may be, according to cause–effect, compare–contrast, sequential order, or description structures. At first you may need to prompt students by reminding them of the text structure. For example, you might say, "Jake, in this selection about volcanoes, we learn about the different causes of volcanoes and the effects they have on the environment. Why don't you go ahead and tell me the important ideas you read about."

Retellings of both narrative and expository text can yield rich information about (1) what students perceive to be important in text, (2) how they organize information during and after reading, and (3) how they share their understanding. It is wise, however, for teachers to remember that no two retellings are alike; each retelling is contingent on each student's interpretation of the text according to his or her own background knowledge and experiences. In this way, retelling is "messy data" (Rhodes & Shanklin, 1993, p. 232), but the process is potentially revealing.

Anecdotal Records and Observational Checklists

We described anecdotal records and observational checklists earlier as they relate to word knowledge, and, as you might expect, you can also use anecdotal records and observational checklists to assess comprehension. Say, for example, that you have modeled the behaviors that you expect of good second-grade readers, such as making predictions before, during, and after reading, summarizing while reading, making connections, and visualizing (Caldwell, 2002). You might develop a checklist that identifies the behaviors you have taught your students. For example, if you have taught your students to do a "picture walk" before reading, you might observe students as they choose a book and see what they do as they get ready to read. You can complete this form of assessment individually, in a reading conference, or you can roam around your classroom as children engage in sustained silent reading or buddy reading. In Figure 4.13 we present one example of a checklist used by a teacher as she observed children working in peer-led discussion groups.

Using Rubrics to Assess Comprehension

You can also use rubrics to assess your students' comprehension strategies. As defined by Winograd et al. (2003), a rubric is a set of descriptions or characteristics that identifies the qualities of good work. A rubric can be very simple: for example, criteria that determine what a student has learned or accomplished in a certain area. Or the rubric can be more elaborate, describing various levels of achievement in a certain area in detail. A more detailed rubric can also include examples of responses corresponding to each level of performance. A rubric, like an observational checklist, can be designed for any task that is used to assess literate behavior.

Date: _____

Book Talk Behaviors

Child	Gets the floor in appropriate ways	Participates in discussion	Connects ideas to text (T), to self (S), or to World (W)	Compares/ contrasts events or ideas in one text to other texts	Builds on ideas of other group members	Uses new vocabulary or concepts in discussion

FIGURE 4.13. Teacher observation form.

From *Teaching Literacy in Second Grade* by Jeanne R. Paratore and Rachel L. McCormack. Copyright 2005 by The Guilford Press. Permission to photocopy this figure is granted to purchasers of this book for personal use only (see copyright page for details).

Rubrics can be designed by teachers after carefully considering the standards students must meet; alternatively, students and teachers can design rubrics together, and the students can use the rubrics to guide and self-assess their performance. Cooper and Kiger (2005) suggest that teachers (1) share rubrics with their students at the beginning of each task, (2) make sure that they know what each part means, (3) encourage them to refer to the rubric throughout the task, and (4) give them an opportunity to use the rubric to evaluate themselves.

Second-grade students are capable of engaging in self-assessment. They can assess their own performance by using checklists and rubrics similar to the ones teachers devise for themselves. For example, if the teacher designs a checklist for retelling, he or she can also make one available for the students. As pairs of students read to each other and retell what they have read, they can check off the parts of the story they heard their partners tell. Engaging students in the assessment process makes the process more transparent and builds awareness and ownership of goals and the ways to accomplish them.

Assessing Writing

In assessing students' writing, experts recommend a dual focus: What do students know about the writing process, and what is their facility with the conventions of language? Many of the previously described assessment strategies are also useful in examining students' writing knowledge. Checklists and anecdotal records can be useful in guiding observation of students' engagement in the stages of the writing process:

What strategies do they use as they plan, draft, revise, and edit?

What does their product reveal about their understanding of the elements of a particular genre, their awareness of audience, their knowledge of grammar and punctuation?

Rubrics, too, can be especially helpful to guide teacher and student evaluation of students' use of focal skills and strategies. Figures 4.14 and 4.15 are examples of rubrics second-grade teachers have used with their students.

HOW DO I MAKE SENSE OF ALL THE INFORMATION?

The assessments described in the previous sections are purposeful and meaningful ways in which to ascertain what your students know about reading and writing.

Name: _____   Date: _____

Checklist for "All about Me" Compositions

Checkmark each sentence that is true. If not, *fix it!*

- I planned my composition using a "web."
- I wrote an exciting lead that grabs my audience.
- I expressed my feelings.
- I used grown-up words.
- I organized my composition into three good paragraphs.
- I indented each paragraph.
- I connected my ending or "clincher" to the lead.
- I used correct punctuation.
- I used correct capitalization.
- I used correct spelling.
- I tried my best to make my composition look neat.

FIGURE 4.14. Sample writing rubric.

From *Teaching Literacy in Second Grade* by Jeanne R. Paratore and Rachel L. McCormack. Copyright 2005 by The Guilford Press. Permission to photocopy this figure is granted to purchasers of this book for personal use only (see copyright page for details).

But for many teachers, collecting information about students' reading and writing performances is relatively easy to do. Working out a way to organize and interpret the multiple assessments so that the evidence can be used to guide instruction can be far more challenging. Literacy portfolios provide one way for teachers and students to work together to make sense of all the information.

What Is a Literacy Portfolio?

Simply stated, a portfolio is a collection of artifacts representing student growth in reading and writing over time. It is a systematic and organized means of collecting data (e.g., student work samples, teacher observations, formal and informal test scores), and it can readily be tied to standards and objectives set by a teacher, school, district, or state. Most important, it is a collaboration between students and their teachers.

Name: _____   Date: _____

Title of Piece: _____

Personal Narrative Rubric and Checklist

Place a checkmark before each sentence that best describes your composition. If it isn't in the "4" category, fix it!

4

- ☐ I wrote an exciting lead.
- ☐ I organized my composition into good paragraphs.
- ☐ I used rich details.
- ☐ I used great words.
- ☐ It is an appropriate length. I told the whole story.
- ☐ I connected the ending sentence to the lead.
- ☐ I used correct grammar.
- ☐ I used correct punctuation.
- ☐ I used correct spelling.

3

- ☐ I wrote a good lead.
- ☐ I organized my composition into paragraphs.
- ☐ I used good details.
- ☐ I used good words.
- ☐ It is an appropriate length. I told the whole story.
- ☐ I connected the ending sentence to the lead.
- ☐ I used mostly correct grammar.
- ☐ I used mostly correct punctuation.
- ☐ I used mostly correct spelling.

2

- ☐ I wrote a poor lead.
- ☐ I did not organize my composition into paragraphs.
- ☐ I used some details.
- ☐ I used ordinary words.
- ☐ It is an inappropriate length. I did not tell the whole story.
- ☐ I did not connect the ending sentence to the lead.
- ☐ I used lots of incorrect grammar.
- ☐ I used lots of incorrect punctuation.
- ☐ I used lots of incorrect spelling.

1

- ☐ I did not write a lead.
- ☐ I used no organization.
- ☐ I used little or no details.
- ☐ I used poor word choice.
- ☐ I did not tell the whole story.
- ☐ I have no ending.
- ☐ I have too many mistakes in grammar.
- ☐ I have too many mistakes in punctuation.
- ☐ I have too many mistakes in spelling.

FIGURE 4.15. Sample writing rubric.

From *Teaching Literacy in Second Grade* by Jeanne R. Paratore and Rachel L. McCormack. Copyright 2005 by The Guilford Press. Permission to photocopy this figure is granted to purchasers of this book for personal use only (see copyright page for details).

What Does a Literacy Portfolio Look Like?

Although portfolio assessment is a concept (collecting performance-based evidence over time), it is also an object: a container or a place in which students and teachers store evidence of students' learning. The particular container or place can vary: a Portfolio can be a folder, a binder, or a crate. It can also be electronic.

We have seen teachers use creative ways to collect and store student work. In one of our graduate classes, we asked our 24 students to each design an organized collection system that allowed easy access for them and their students to select, store, analyze, and review student work samples that reflected their students' literacy behaviors. The assignment resulted in 24 unique ways that reflected the individual teacher's interpretation of the task.

What Should Be Included in Portfolios?

Portfolios should include work samples that are *formative* (showing progress or growth) and *summative* (showing achievement). In essence, you can include anything that demonstrates what the student has learned and is able to do.

A typical second-grade portfolio might include some combination of the following items:

➢ Attitude and interest survey given at the beginning of the year

➢ A book log (current month or term)

➢ A book log self-assessment sheet (from last month or term, with goals)

➢ A book project or photo of project

➢ Running records that have been shared and discussed with students

➢ Story retelling in pictures, words, or sound recording

➢ Story maps and other graphic organizers

➢ Checklists for decoding and comprehension strategies

➢ Writing samples—final drafts

➢ Scoring rubrics and checklists generated by teachers and students

An additional writing folder might contain the following:

➢ A list of student-generated writing topics

➢ Writing samples in various stages of the writing process

➢ Finished pieces with scoring rubrics or checklists attached

How Should I Get Started?

The process of planning and implementing a portfolio system has been widely explored in the literature. The suggestions we make here have been drawn from two sources: David Cooper and N. D. Kiger (2005) and Joanne Caldwell (2002).

1. Introduce the concept of portfolios to your students and their parents. Parents and families especially need to know about the use of portfolios in your classrooms. Parents often expect their children to bring papers home every day—evidence of what their children have been doing in school. If your procedure includes collecting and storing some of the students' daily work and assessment samples, families need to be informed. You can provide this information in a letter home that is sent to parents, or during open house if you have a regularly scheduled meeting at the beginning of the school year.

2. Show your students an example. If you typically use portfolios, you may have one from the previous year. If not, ask a colleague if he or she uses portfolios and can lend you one to show to your students. Another option is to show a portfolio that you are keeping as evidence of your own learning.

3. Identify the categories that will be included. For a literacy portfolio, you may want to start with attitudes and interests, word identification, and comprehension. Start with a few categories until you and your students feel comfortable.

4. Identify the standards set by your school, district, or state. The artifacts you and your students collect should demonstrate how they are working toward meeting those standards.

5. Establish procedures for (a) selecting artifacts, (b) placing them in the portfolio containers, (c) writing an entry or self-reflection, (d) determining how to use the portfolios as part of a conference with parents, and (e) determining when to review, clean out, and reevaluate the contents. Review your goals and ask the students to choose which pieces most reflect their growth toward meeting those goals.

6. Plan regular times to review the portfolios with your students. You may want to guide your students to review the contents of their portfolios once a month or once a term. One teacher we observed used Friday afternoons to talk about the portfolios, review the artifacts, and set goals for the next week.

How Do I Use Portfolios to Report Progress?

Portfolios are very useful during parent–teacher conferences. You might use the portfolio to identify "talking points" during conferences that highlight the students' progress. One teacher with whom we work commented that her parent conferences took on a whole different tone once she started using portfolios; she had a new frame for her remarks to parents and she was able to demonstrate the progress their children were making.

Another teacher we work with uses portfolios as part of parent–child–teacher conferences. She coaches her students on how to describe each portfolio sample. Each spring she holds a Portfolio Showcase to which she invites families, colleagues, administration, and members of the community to visit the classroom; the students stand by their portfolios and talk about them.

A CLASSROOM VISIT

Shauna DiLuca teaches second grade on the island of Nantucket, Massachusetts. There are 16 children in her classroom, all general education students, with the exception of one student who is identified as having special learning needs and has an individual educational plan. Shauna is in her fourth year of teaching. During the past year she has focused particularly on improving the ways in which she uses informal assessments to understand her students' literacy needs. We asked her to walk us through the types of assessment she uses from the beginning to the end of the school year, and to explain how and why she uses each.

Shauna explained that she begins the year by administering an attitude and interest survey so that she can get to know her students and learn about topics that might be especially engaging and motivating for them. She administers the survey as a whole-class activity, guiding children through each question. As the children record their responses, she circulates and provides assistance to any child who seems to be confused by the task or the question. At the end of the day, she reviews her children's responses and makes a list of the topics they listed as special interests. Then she reviews the collection of books she has in her classroom library and sorts some of the books into "special" baskets. These baskets are labeled with topics that her children have highlighted as interests. She also makes notes about topics of interest for which she has few or no books, so that she can visit the school library and borrow some books that will engage children right from the start. The next day, during the morning meeting, she explains to her children that she read what they had written about their reading interests, and she shows the students the special baskets of books she has assembled. During the first few weeks of school, she makes a point of choosing a book from one of these baskets to read aloud. She encourages children who did not name this particular topic as an interest to choose one of the books from the focal basket as one of their own reading choices to see if it is a topic that they, too, might like to read about.

Because Shauna is always concerned with helping her students develop both reading fluency and a love of reading, she gives them extended, uninterrupted time during the day to self-select books and read. She also encourages her students to read independently at home. Shauna's students read a lot, so she shows them how to log the books they read independently in a book log. She models the logging process, using books she has read on her own, and then she guides them through the process by having them begin to log the last book they have read. Each day she reminds her students to log any books they have read at home and in school during independent reading time.

By the second week of school, Shauna administers a metacognitive awareness interview, one child at a time, to assess her students' understanding of reading and writing strategies. She calls each student to a small table in the classroom and explains that she will be asking him or her questions about the kinds of things he or she thinks about and does as he or she reads and writes. As she asks the student each question, she jots down his or her responses. Shauna knows that at the beginning of second grade, her students are really more like first graders; she often has to rephrase the questions she asks. For example, Shauna might ask the student, "What do you do before you begin to read a book?" She sometimes has to rephrase her question by asking, "How do you get your mind ready to read?"

Administering this survey is a priority for Shauna, so when her students are engaged in learning center activities, she devotes some of her small-group instruction time to interviewing each child. It takes a few days, says Shauna, but this interview gives her a wealth of information about her students. After each child has been interviewed, Shauna looks at their responses and asks herself many questions:

What do my students know about being good readers and writers?

What self-monitoring strategies do they know? What do they think good readers do?

What do they think good writers do?

What strategies do I have to teach?

Based on the answers to her questions, Shauna plans her instruction. For example, if she finds that most of her students are not able to tell her what they do before they read a book (make predictions, do a picture walk, think about what they already know about the topic), Shauna knows that those strategies will be her first focus: She will model those strategies during shared reading and provide guided practice during guided reading groups.

Shauna takes running records of her students during the first few weeks. She is required by her district to track her students' progress in reading by taking a running record of benchmark passages three times during the year: in September, January, and May. In September, Shauna has students read a 100-word passage of a text that is typical of a beginning second-grade reader. After analyzing the results of the running records, she is able to get a quick glimpse of the range of abilities in her classroom. These results help her match children to appropriate texts for guided reading groups. Shauna begins these groups by the third week of school. She typically has three groups, which are easily managed during her learning center time. She assesses these groups frequently to track each student's progress and, more importantly, to adjust her groups whenever necessary.

Running records are taken for another important reason at the beginning of the year and at various points during the weeks and months that follow. Because Shauna also uses grade-level core texts for her community reading and content-area subjects, she periodically selects a 100-word passage from these texts and assesses each student's reading accuracy. In this way, she can determine how she can help each student read and understand the text. This practice takes time, Shauna notes, but yields a great deal of information. As you might expect, Shauna typically finds that some students can read the content-area texts independently; some may need support from an abler peer and need to "buddy read" the text; still others need to have the texts read by the teacher before attempting to read it independently.

Throughout the school year Shauna assesses her students' understanding of texts in many ways: through informal observation of reading behaviors, which she documents on a checklist; through an assessment of think-alouds during reading conferences; through questioning, both written and oral; through oral retellings documented on a checklist; and through art and book projects. Examples from these methods become part of each student's literacy portfolio.

Student portfolios also contain samples of student writing. Shauna asks students to include writing samples from different genres, and she devises rubrics tied to the state standards. Some of the rubrics, however, are student generated. Shauna also collaborates with the other second-grade teachers to design criteria for her students' performance in writing.

Students choose work samples for their portfolios that exhibit their growth over time. Shauna confers with a few students every day about the pieces to include in the portfolios. She asks the students to consider: Does this piece show that you are meeting, or trying to meet, our goals? Do the pieces show how you are improving over time? Because the students cannot store all of their work in the portfolios, Shauna shows them how to choose the ones that best answer her questions. Each piece of evidence is attached to a sheet of paper that says: "I chose this for my portfolio because. . . . " Shauna's students store their artifacts in colorful plastic accordion folders that have several pockets labeled "My Interests," "My Reading," "My Writing," and "My Projects." These are kept in large plastic crates that are accessible to all students. Shauna's students say that the portfolios make them "feel important." They recognize that the portfolios contain worthwhile artifacts and significant information about them.

Shauna uses the portfolios at parent conferences as she talks with the parents about their children's progress. This year Shauna wants to include her students in the conferences by letting them talk about what they are learning in school. She plans to have the students use the portfolio as a prop to guide their discussions.

Shauna told us that her portfolios are still a work-in-progress. Because she took a graduate course in authentic assessment last year, she was required to develop, try, and implement many different kinds of classroom literacy assessments over a short period of time. She is beginning to feel more comfortable as she tries each one again and refines her procedures for assessing and interpreting them. "Start slowly," Shauna warns. "It's a lot of work, but it's worth it."

LOOKING BACKWARD AND FORWARD

In this chapter we described ways in which skillful second-grade teachers use assessment techniques to guide and focus instruction. Our visit with Shauna DiLuca showed us ways in which a comparatively inexperienced teacher can get started with authentic, classroom-based assessment, including portfolio use. In Chapter 5 we continue our journey to excellent teaching, this time exploring the ways effective teachers use their knowledge of literacy learning and their knowledge of their particular students to plan instruction that is responsive to children's individual learning needs.

Try It Out

1. Make a list of your current assessment routines. About which areas of reading and writing knowledge do your routines provide detailed information? What areas are left relatively unexamined? Look back at the chapter and identify particular assessments that you might add to your repertoire to provide a more complete profile of children's literacy performance. Choose one and consider how you might integrate it within your instructional routines. Try it out and discuss what you learn about your students with a teaching colleague.

2. Would you like to start a portfolio system? Consider how you might get started. To begin, choose some form of storage container and one or two assessment practices. For example, many teachers begin with the book log. Provide time each day for children to record the books they have read; at the end of a week or two, ask children to look back over the list and reflect on the books. Which did they like best? Least? Which would they recommend to a friend and why? What would they like to read next? After you and your students are comfortable with the book-log routine, add a new assessment practice to the portfolio. As you and your students gain comfort with each new practice, consider what you might do next to continue to deepen your (and their) understanding.

3. If you are not familiar with, or skilled at, giving running records, check the list of resources in Chapter 8 for those that are helpful in learning this assessment practice.

CHAPTER 5

DIFFERENTIATING INSTRUCTION FOR DIVERSE LEARNERS

I n this chapter we examine the complex issue of how excellent teachers respond to the individual differences they uncover through good assessment. We have organized the chapter to address two primary topics. One is how teachers group students for instruction, and in the first section we examine what we know about the effects of various grouping plans. The second topic is the instructional needs of children who struggle in reading and writing. In that section we address the types of instructional practices or strategies that have proven to be helpful in meeting the needs of special learners. As in earlier chapters, we begin by examining the research evidence bearing on each topic and then apply that to classroom practice.

A BRIEF HISTORY OF GROUPING PRACTICES

Over the last several years, grouping practices in elementary classrooms have undergone a series of transformations. During the 1950s, 1960s, 1970s, and through much of 1980s, most classroom teachers organized children for reading instruction within predominantly static ability groups (Barr & Dreeben, 1983). This seems to make good sense: If children entered our classrooms with varied levels of reading proficiency, then we would best meet their needs by choosing instructional texts closely matched to their current level of reading proficiency.

However, evidence of unexpected negative consequences of ability grouping began to mount. Research conducted over the course of nearly 30 years indicated that when students were taught predominantly in groups formed on the basis of reading ability, consistently negative outcomes were observed: Children in the lowest-performing groups maintained their low rates of performance and the gap between high- and low-performing students increased (Good & Marshall, 1984; Slavin, 1987). In addition, researchers discovered that these results could be explained at least partially by differential approaches to instruction offered to learners of high and low ability. In separate analyses of existing evidence, Allington (1983b) and Hiebert (1983) reported that children in low-performing groups received qualitatively different instructional experiences, including reading half as many in-context words, fewer opportunities to write, fewer opportunities for discussion, and fewer opportunities to respond to critical thinking questions.

A second factor that influenced classroom grouping practices related to what has sometimes been called the "whole-language movement." Whereas basal reading programs were largely associated with the practice of ability grouping, the whole-language approach (which emphasized the use of authentic and original literature) was associated with whole-class instruction. A hallmark of the whole-language approach—the practice of "shared reading," in which teachers read selections aloud to children or in which teachers and children read selections chorally—was easily implemented within whole-class settings, and it became popular as a way to provide low-performing readers with access to difficult text. In addition, the practice of "every child on the same page" was embraced as a way to build a more inclusive community of learners, in which all children have equal access to high-quality texts and high-quality teaching.

As a result, throughout much of the 1990s, whether teachers chose the basal reading approach or the whole-language approach, many favored the practice of whole-group instruction. Toward the end of the 1990s, however, research on the practice of using *no* grouping at all began to emerge. Experimental studies that systematically compared ability grouping to whole-class instruction found conclusive results favoring ability grouping over no grouping at all, with positive findings related to achievement, attitude, and self-concept (Lou et al., 1996). The research findings were consistent with the observations of many teachers, who had observed that although children benefited from the inclusiveness of whole-class instruction and the opportunity to listen and respond to good literature, they did not actually learn to *read* the texts.

When teachers are confronted with these two bodies of evidence, many are understandably confused and even frustrated. Neither approach seems to serve children well. Is our choice, then, one of selecting the lesser of two evils? Or is there a more thoughtful approach to grouping lurking somewhere around the edges? In fact, when we look beyond the two major types of grouping, we find that there is yet other evidence that is instructive.

In addition to the practices of ability grouping and whole-class instruction, two other types of grouping have been widely studied, but less often used for the teaching of reading. Investigations of *cooperative learning*, the practice of forming heterogeneous, student-led groups, and *peer tutoring*, the practice of forming student dyads, indicate promising learning effects. In the area of cooperative learning, researchers (e.g., Johnson, Maruyama, Johnson, & Nelson, 1981; Sharan, 1980; Slavin, 1980) report that students of all ability levels who work in cooperative learning groups do better than their peers who work in traditional groups. An examination of the contexts in which these studies were conducted indicates that the learning tasks were largely focused on acquisition of ideas and concepts, rather than acquisition of particular skills and strategies. That is, students worked within cooperative groups for purposes of exploration, problem solving, or discussion rather than to advance a specific reading skill or ability.

In the case of peer tutoring, studies (e.g., Cohen, Kulik, & Kulik, 1982) support a conclusion that this grouping practice can lead to higher levels of achievement for both members of tutoring dyads, but that such effects are likely to be realized only when the learning task is highly structured and explicit in nature and measured with an instrument highly congruent with the learning activity. In contrast to cooperative learning groups, peer dyads were highly successful when they were focused on specific skill development.

As researchers and teachers have reviewed the evidence on the full range of grouping practices, many have believed that the answer to effective classroom practice would not be found in the implementation of any one type of grouping, but rather in the use of multiple forms of grouping. Various instructional designs comprising some combination of large and small groups, including both needs-based and multi-ability combinations, have been implemented and tested. Although related studies are relatively few in number and primarily nonexperimental in design, they offer encouraging preliminary results.

First, when looking at studies that have measured reading achievement in traditional ways—that is, through the administration of either achievement tests or informal reading inventories—the results are largely consistent across all of the studies. When organized for reading instruction according to grouping practices that abandon the traditional, static, ability grouping framework, students at all levels of ability achieve at higher levels on measures of reading vocabulary, reading comprehension, and reading fluency (Cunningham, Hall, & Defee, 1991; Hall & Cunningham, 1996; Jenkins et al., 1994; Stevens, Madden, Slavin, & Farnish, 1987; Stevens & Slavin, 1995; Turpie & Paratore, 1995). Second, when nontraditional measures of reading achievement are considered, such as the ways in which children demonstrate understanding through group discussions and assume leadership during discussions, evidence again supports the effectiveness of heterogeneous grouping in the teaching of reading (Goatley, Brock, & Raphael, 1995; Raphael, Brock, & Wallace, 1996; Raphael & Brock, 1993).

Of critical importance in reviewing the evidence, however, is the comprehensive, varied, and flexible nature of the instructional framework within each of the studies in question. In addition to varying the grouping practices used in the classroom, each of the studies provided students with (1) intensive instruction in word study, (2) many opportunities to read and reread text individually and with others, (3) many opportunities to write both in response to text and in contexts unrelated to their reading texts, and (4) many opportunities to engage in oral discussions with their peers.

Furthermore, the nature of the various instructional opportunities is important. In no case, for example, were children who were struggling readers expected to contend with difficult text on their own. Instead, each of the studies utilized a variety of strategies to help children negotiate difficult text. Included were teacher read-alouds, opportunities for individual and paired rereadings, intensive instruction and practice in word study, and practice reading easy text. In addition, in some of the classrooms students who were struggling were provided pull-out instruction in direct support of the classroom activities, and in some cases in-class support directly related to regular education tasks was provided. In some studies, children who were advanced readers were given daily opportunities to read text at more challenging levels and, in some cases, to serve as peer or cross-age tutors. In short, in no case did the instructional model represent a "one-size-fits-all" framework.

Our understanding of the combined evidence on the effects of various grouping practices leads us to a simple claim: How we group students certainly matters, but what we do within the various groups also matters. That is, the various studies suggest that students are affected not only by the ways in which they are grouped but also by the instructional experiences and opportunities they receive within each group. In the next section we review evidence that helps us understand the instructional needs of children who struggle to learn to read and write.

INSTRUCTIONAL PRACTICES THAT MEET THE NEEDS OF SPECIAL LEARNERS

To gain a clear understanding of the instructional needs of poor readers, some researchers have pursued what has been called a "good reader/poor reader" line of research. That is, researchers (e.g., Stanovich, 2000) have attempted to identify the characteristics that differentiate good from poor readers and then to determine if direct, explicit instruction in skills or strategies that poor readers lack, in fact, results in higher levels of reading achievement. Parts of the results are largely predictable. For example, the evidence indicates that good readers are better at (1) word segmentation and blending, (2) reading words in isolation and in context, including the accuracy and fluency with which they read words, and (3) comprehending and remembering what they read. However, other findings are less predictable and may be especially useful in explaining these differences. In particular, researchers have found that low-performing readers commonly have less well-developed language knowledge, are less sensitive to text structure, are less likely to monitor their comprehension, and are more likely to approach text passively. Most importantly, intervention studies indicate that when these needs are explicitly and strategically addressed through carefully planned and expertly implemented instruction, students' reading performance improves.

Taken together, the evidence convinces us that meeting individual needs is not simply a practice of differentiating instruction by placing children in different book levels. Rather, meeting individual needs also requires that we understand that children need to be taught to approach the reading task in particular ways. When we think of children who struggle, we typically think of their need to develop more effective word-reading abilities. However, by itself, proficient word reading will not enable skilled reading. In addition to more explicit and intensive instruction in word-reading accuracy and fluency, some children also need to be exposed to texts and experiences that expand their vocabulary and language knowledge; some children need instruction in how to set purposes for reading; some need to know before they read what text structure to expect and how to use their awareness of text structure to support their understanding of the text; and some need to be taught how to monitor their reading comprehension and how to "fix up" when their understanding breaks down.

FROM RESEARCH TO PRACTICE: PLANNING INSTRUCTION IN A MULTIPLY-GROUPED CLASSROOM

How can teachers make sense of this information in the context of their own classrooms? Given that different types of groups meet different types of learning needs, best practice is achieved when teachers use combinations of grouping options, strategically choosing a particular grouping type in response to children's specific learning needs. For example:

> *Whole-class instruction* is especially effective when the purpose is to introduce ideas, concepts, skills, or strategies that are new to all, or almost all, of the children in a classroom.

> *Teacher-led homogeneous groups* are beneficial when a small group of students needs instruction, review, or additional practice in particular skills and strategies.

> *Student-led heterogeneous groups or dyads* provide effective settings for practice and application of previously taught information.

> *Individual response* allows opportunities for students to use and apply skills and strategies in independent work.

As we understand the evidence, best practice occurs when teachers use *multiple grouping*, a label that we chose to underscore the principle that if *all* children are to become successful and accomplished readers, teachers need to involve students in more than one type of reading group. What might a typical day in a multiply-grouped second-grade classroom look like? The multiple-grouping model developed by Paratore (2000) is framed by three daily literacy events: community reading, just-right reading, and on-your-own reading (Figure 5.1). During each of these literacy events, the particular reading texts, teaching activities, and student tasks are chosen to respond to what we have learned about the needs of different readers.

Community reading

• Time each day when children read (or listen to) grade-appropriate text

Just-right reading

• Time each day when children receive instruction in text that will support the development of particular word-level and comprehension strategies

On-your-own reading

• Time each day when children read anything of their own choosing

---

FIGURE 5.1. Typical day in a multiply-grouped classroom.

Community Reading

In community reading, children read or listen and respond to text that will support the development of language and concepts appropriate at their grade level. Community reading is intended to achieve two major purposes. The first is to provide every child with access to grade-appropriate curriculum, and by so doing, to provide opportunities for every child to acquire grade-appropriate vocabulary, concepts, and language structures. The second purpose is to create contexts that support the development of the classroom as a learning community, where a focus on the same text or

topic by children of different ability levels enables all children to interact and provides an opportunity for them to learn from one another. In classrooms where teachers use a basal reading program, children may read a selection from the anthology during the community reading time period. In classrooms where tradebooks frame the reading program, children generally read a teacher-selected tradebook or choose from a selection of thematically related tradebooks during this time period. Because all children read the same text, or a collection of texts, about the same topic or theme during this particular time period, these lessons typically begin with whole-class instruction, during which children prepare for reading by making predictions, reviewing key vocabulary and concepts, and posing questions. Although time allocations differ in every classroom, on average, teachers allocate about 45–60 minutes to the community reading component of the literacy program.

During the period when children read text, small groups are usually formed on the basis of children's reading needs. In one group, children who are capable readers are directed to read the text on their own and to complete a teacher-assigned cooperative learning activity. The assigned task is selected precisely to motivate students to reflect on, and respond to, the text in ways that will clarify meaning or challenge their thinking. In choosing the comprehension tasks, we are guided, in particular, by three criteria. First, the tasks we assign must be consistent with strategies previously taught. For example, after we have provided explicit instruction in story mapping to the whole class, we might ask children to work with partners to construct a story map of the next story. Second, the tasks we assign must also engage students in higher-level thinking. So, for example, after constructing a story map, we might ask students to consider the connection between a character's actions and story outcomes. What if the character had acted differently? How would that different behavior have changed the outcome? Third, we plan comprehension activities that we expect could be useful to students during subsequent lessons. For example, students might save story maps in a journal or notebook and, after a few weeks, review their collection of maps and compare and contrast events or characters.

In another group the teacher may assist struggling readers. For some children, grade-level text represents "frustration level" material, and without teacher guidance and support, some students are likely to fail. In these cases, the teacher's responsibility is to mediate text difficulty in ways that prevent frustration. That is, the teacher must intervene with strategies and practices that make the text readable. Such intervention strategies include (1) reading all or part of the text aloud before children are expected to read it on their own; (2) providing instruction in vocabulary that is essential to comprehending the selection; (3) engaging children

in choral or echo readings; or (4) by assigning buddy reading. Students who need to develop word-reading accuracy and fluency may be given additional opportunities to reread parts or all of the text individually, with a partner, or with the teacher. After children have finished reading the text, they work with the teacher to complete the same comprehension task their higher-performing peers completed on their own or in small groups. In the teacher-led lesson, struggling readers are given more explicit instruction when required by the text. That is, they may be reminded of text structure and guided to use the structure in recalling or retelling important ideas. Or the teacher may focus on specific vocabulary, concepts, or language structures and discuss how the writing style influences their understanding of the text.

After all children have read and responded to the text, the groups reconvene as a whole class or as small heterogeneous groups to share what they have read and learned that day. In many classrooms, this is the time when literature circles (Short & Pierce, 1998) or book clubs (Raphael & McMahon, 1997) are conducted. Figure 5.2 provides a graphic representation of the community reading segment of daily literacy instruction.

Just-Right Reading

In the just-right reading period, small groups are formed to provide children with instruction in text that is "just right" for them—that is, text that they can read with

---

Story Introduction (Whole Class)

- Preview text, develop background knowledge, make predictions

Reading the Selection (Needs-Based Groups)

No Help	*With Help (Teacher-Led Group)*
• Silent reading	• Read-aloud by teacher
• Partner reading	• Rereading with teacher or partner
• Partner response (oral)	• Group response (oral)
• Individual response (written)	• Individual response (written)

Responding to the Selection (Heterogeneous Groups or Whole Class)

- Literature circles or large-group discussion or strategy lesson

---

FIGURE 5.2. Community reading.

90–95% accuracy, a level that is widely believed to be optimal for acquiring word knowledge, fluency, and accuracy (Juel, 1988, 1990; Clay, 1979). Just-right reading groups are usually small (four to eight children) and typically last for 20 minutes or so. Instructional models such as those developed by Taylor, Strait, and Medo (1994), Hiebert (1994), and Jackson, Paratore, Chard, and Garnick (1999) are especially appropriate for struggling readers. Each of these models is group based, which allows the teacher to work with more than one child at a time. In addition, each model includes three important tasks in each lesson: reading a focal book, engaging in systematic and explicit word study, and rereading familiar books.

For able and advanced readers, the just-right reading period offers opportunities to return to the text used during community reading for explicit instruction in word-level or comprehension strategies, or, when appropriate, to read beyond the grade-level text and receive instruction that will challenge them cognitively, linguistically, and motivationally. Figure 5.3 presents a graphic representation of just-right reading.

On-Your-Own Reading

On-your-own reading (Figure 5.4) encompasses activities more widely known as sustained silent reading (McCracken & McCracken, 1978) or "drop everything and read" (Ziegler, 1993). It is the time of day when children choose to read any book or text of interest to them, and if they wish, to share their responses with teacher and peers. On average, teachers allocate about 15 minutes each day to student-selected reading of this type.

In summary, community reading might be considered the part of literacy instruction that is driven by the grade-level curriculum—the time when the focal text is important not only for the reading lessons that accompany it, but also for the language, concepts, and content lessons embedded within it. It is participation in community reading that protects lower-performing readers from being tracked in low-level reading materials that

Supporting Struggling Readers

- Instruction in word-level strategies using easy text
- Reading and rereading of easy books

Supporting Average and Above-Average Readers

- Instruction in word-level and comprehension strategies using community reading text
- Reading beyond community reading text
- Serving as peer or cross-age tutor

FIGURE 5.3. Just-right reading.

- Children read a book or text of their own choosing.
- Children may read individually or in pairs.
- Teacher may intervene if child consistently or repeatedly chooses books that are too easy or too difficult.

FIGURE 5.4. On-your-own reading.

historically have denied them access to the language, concepts, and vocabulary necessary for success at their grade level. *Just-right reading* represents that part of literacy instruction that is driven by the teacher and his or her expert knowledge of each individual's reading needs. Consistent with the Vygotskian (1978) notion of the zone of proximal development, the teacher chooses text that is within each child's reach when working with a teacher; that is, text that the child can read with effective and appropriate instruction and scaffolding. *On-your-own* reading represents the part of the literacy program that is driven by the child; it is a response to evidence that motivation for reading and self-directedness comes, at least partially, from having the opportunity to make choices along the way (Guthrie, Alvermann, & Au, 1998; Guthrie & Wigfield, 1999).

Managing a Multiply-Grouped Literacy Classroom

Effective management of a multiply grouped classroom requires special attention to four ideas addressed in earlier chapters. In Chapter 3, in our discussion of the characteristics of classrooms where children excel in reading and writing, we noted the importance of reliable and consistent daily routines and the presence of centers in which students can work productively when working alone or in small student-led groups. In Chapter 2 we described and provided examples of explicit and strategic instruction in both decoding and comprehension. In Chapter 4 we presented strategies for trustworthy and ongoing assessment and monitoring of students' learning. Because each of these ideas is especially important to effective implementation of a multiply-grouped literacy classroom, we return to them now and discuss each in relation to the successful management of multiple reading groups.

Consistent Daily Routines

In classrooms where multiple grouping is effective, day-to-day activities are highly structured and consistent, and children can largely predict what will happen each day. For example, children know that each day they will engage in reading and rereading of text, and if these tasks involve reading with a partner, they also will be told explicitly what is expected of them during this activity. Although there are a number of ways to implement what has become widely known as buddy or partner reading, in many classrooms children alternate pages with the understanding that while their partner is reading, they must follow along so that they can assist with unknown words. We especially like the practice of asking children to use their "three-step voice," a voice that the teacher cannot hear if she takes three small steps away from the reading buddies. This strategy has been effective in helping even very young children to lower their voices as they read aloud.

Similarly, children know that each day they will engage in the task of writing responses to what they have read. They have reading journals readily accessible to them in their desks, and they know the routines for completing and submitting their work. In addition, they are fully aware of how to seek help from the teacher or a peer when they are unclear or confused about an assignment. And finally, children know what to do when they finish their work—how to check it, where to put it, and what to do next.

Explicit Instruction

In a multiply-grouped classroom children routinely spend some period of time working alone, with a partner, or in peer-led groups. In classrooms where children do so successfully, they are familiar with the strategies they have been asked to implement during these times. Typically, the teacher has systematically and explicitly taught the focal strategy and used the gradual release model (Pearson & Gallagher, 1983), providing demonstration, guided practice, and independent application in previous teacher-led lessons. So, for example, if children are expected to meet with a group to compose a story summary, the teacher might have spent time with the whole group completing a story map on a shared story and using the story map to compose a group summary. Then the teacher might have asked children to use the strategy on their own, and carefully monitored their products to ascertain their understanding and facility with the strategy. Having done so, the teacher can safely conclude that the children can apply the strategy on their own or within a student-led group setting.

Monitoring Children's Performance

Effective implementation of multiple grouping requires that teachers engage in daily "kidwatching" (Goodman, 1982), observing children during all phases of the literacy program to make certain that they are both supported and challenged. Monitoring strategies might include the frequent use of running records (Clay, 1979) taken while reading with children individually or "behind their backs" as they are partner reading. Retellings provide information about children's comprehension of the text, their ability to organize their recall, their oral language, and their ability to elaborate and clarify. Listening to children during book talks can also provide information about their comprehension and oral language abilities. In addition, eavesdropping on these conversations can provide teachers with valuable information about children's group participation styles: how they get the floor, how they agree or disagree with their peers, how they justify their point of view, how they clarify confusion. Finally, children's written responses to reading may provide information about phonemic awareness, spelling, comprehension of text, and grammatical understanding.

Learning Center Activities

In multiply-grouped classrooms there are periods of time each day when students are expected to work individually or with their peers, without the benefit of the teacher's direct oversight and guidance. Many teachers assign students to learning centers during these periods of time—and in some cases, learning center time can total as much as 30 or 40 minutes a day. It is important that this time is spent on tasks that both engage students *and* have a high likelihood of advancing them to higher levels of reading achievement. Recall the "rules" we set forth in Chapter 3 on setting up centers in which students can be expected to make learning gains:

1. Learning center tasks must be evidence based; that is, credible research must indicate that completing assigned tasks will contribute to children's development as capable readers and writers.

2. Learning center tasks must be accessible to students. Assigned tasks must require use of skills and strategies that have been taught and that students are capable of applying independently.

3. Learning center tasks must be connected in some way to other literacy or content-area studies of the day or week.

Consider these rules as you plan learning center activities for use in your multiply-grouped classroom,

A CLASSROOM VISIT

For this visit we asked Karen Murray, a second-grade teacher in Nantucket, Massachusetts, to "walk us through" one day in her multiply-grouped second-grade classroom in a school that qualifies for Title I funding. There are 17 children in Karen's classroom. Among them is one child who is from El Salvador, one who is from the Dominican Republic, and one who is from Taiwan. The home language for each of these children is either Spanish or Chinese, but only the child from Taiwan receives instruction in English as a second language. Four of the 17 children are identified as having moderate special needs, and one child is identified as having severe special needs.

As you visit Karen's classroom, consider what you have learned about research-based instruction. Can you identify evidence that supports Karen's teaching decisions and actions?

Teachers at Karen's school use a literacy module plan to organize their literacy instruction. The plan loosely follows the guidelines described in the previous section of this chapter and involves three modules: Module A is community reading, module B is just-right reading and learning centers, and module C is interactive language arts. The plan uses a variety of grouping configurations, allows teachers to work with small groups of students who have similar learning needs, and gives students many opportunities for sustained reading practice.

In module A (community reading) teachers use the published anthology or another grade-appropriate text to teach reading to all the students. Some teachers opt to use grade-appropriate trade books representing a variety of genres; at times they may use content-area texts. The instruction in this module follows a pre- during- and postreading organizational structure. Teachers help students get ready to read by building and accessing background information, developing vocabulary, making predictions, and teaching a mini-lesson. Then students read the selection. After reading, the students reflect on, and respond to, the selection.

In module B students are grouped according to similar learning needs to work with the teacher in just-right reading groups. When not working with the teacher, the students work in learning centers. In module C students have writing workshop, interactive writing, and word study. The modules are not meant to be linear; rather, they are offered in different sequences by different teachers. Karen explained that she typically uses an A–C–B pattern.

A Walk-Through of the Three Modules

Module A: Community Reading

Karen gathers her students into the common meeting area, where they sit in front of her on a rug. Karen's objective for the lesson is that her students demonstrate their ability to visualize while reading. The selection she chooses to teach this strategy is *Miss Rumphius* (Cooney, 1982), a story from the second-grade district-adopted anthology. The lyrics of the Louis Armstrong song "What a Wonderful World" are displayed on a chart at the front of the meeting area, and the children begin with a choral reading of it. Karen then asks students, "What do you think a wonderful world would look like?" She writes their responses on a piece of chart paper on the easel.

She introduces the main selection by saying, "The story we will read today is about a person who tries to make the world more beautiful in a very unique way." Karen then writes key terms from the story on the chalkboard: *bristling masts*, *lupines*, *bushels*, *figureheads*. She tells the students that they will see these words in the text, and that she will help them to visualize their meanings while reading and discuss them after they have read the story. As explained in Chapter 2, Karen knows that vocabulary instruction should contain three key elements: meaningful usage, integration into prior knowledge, and repetition (Nagy, 1986).

Karen begins reading aloud from the selection and modeling visualization strategies. For example, when she reads "bristling masts," she thinks aloud and says that a bottle brush or hair brush has bristles, and that from far away, the ships' masts must have looked like brushes. She tells the students that while they read, they should use their own personal experiences to come up with images and visualize the meanings in the story. She explains that visualizing the meanings of new words and concepts is a strategy good readers use to build an understanding as they read.

Because approximately half of Karen's students can read the selection on their own, she stops the demonstration here. She directs the capable readers to read the story independently at their seats or in another quiet area of the classroom. She reminds them to use the visualization strategy when they encounter new words to help clarify the author's meaning. The rest of the class remains at the common meeting area, and Karen continues to read the selection aloud while students follow along in their texts. As she reads, she provides more explicit modeling of the visualization strategy. About half-way through the text, Karen asks the students to join her in reading aloud the remainder of the text. As they encounter the key words Karen has written on the chalkboard, they pause and Karen asks students to volunteer to try the visualization strategy that she has modeled.

When Karen and the small group have completed their reading of the text, the students who have been reading the selection independently join Karen at the common meeting area. They spend a few minutes reacting to the story, and then Karen leads a whole-class discussion of "How would *you* make the world more beautiful?" She adds their suggestions to the chart.

Module C: Interactive Language Arts

The students gather at the Common Meeting area to review and reread the list of ways in which they would make the world a more beautiful place. Then Karen models how to choose one idea and write several sentences about it. She purposely makes some errors in capitalization and punctuation, then demonstrates how she goes back to edit or "fix" her writing. The students are then given an assignment they will complete in module B: "In your journal, tell how you would make the world a more wonderful place to live in. Use the strategies I showed you to edit your writing."

Module B: Just-Right Reading and Learning Centers

Karen's students are grouped according to similar learning needs for module B learning activities. In this module groups of students meet with Karen every 2 or 3 days. While one group meets with Karen for just-right reading, the other groups respond to the prompt they were given during module C. When they are done, they engage in self-selected reading. After about 15 minutes, the groups rotate.

In the just-right reading group, Karen repeats the pre- during- and postreading format. On this particular day, the first group of students reads *The Hole in Harry's Pocket* (Bloksberg, 1995). Karen explained that she chose this book for two reasons: It is consistent with the students' diagnosed reading levels, and it provides many opportunities for them to use the visualization strategy introduced during community reading.

She begins the lesson by reviewing the visualization strategy she modeled in module A. "Remember the reading strategy we learned today: visualization? Now we will practice it while we read this story." She begins by asking the students if they ever had a hole in their pocket and tells them to turn to a partner to tell about it. She then helps them decode some of the words in the selection: *refrigerator, curb, shiny, tightly*. She writes the words on a small table easel, and the students use their word study strategies to segment the words by chunking them into known parts and then blending the parts together. After each word is identified, Karen discusses the word's meaning, then asks the students to read the passage silently. Next, the students read aloud self-selected passages from the story and demonstrate to Karen how they visualized while they read. After reading, Karen asks the students to check their pants, backpacks, or coats and make a list of the various things in their pockets. When they finish, they find a classmate who has also finished and read the list of "found" items to each other.

At the end of this lesson, groups rotate, and Karen follows a similar guided reading procedure with each group.

LOOKING BACKWARD AND FORWARD

In this chapter we continued our discussion of the importance of knowing what to teach, when to teach, and how to teach. We reviewed the research related to grouping practices and to the instructional needs of children who struggle to read and write. Based on our understanding of the evidence, we drew two major conclusions. First, we concluded that children of all learning abilities have the best opportunities to succeed in reading and writing in classrooms in which they participate daily, or almost daily, in multiple reading groups that use multiple types of texts—texts that are (1) grade-appropriate, (2) matched to students' reading proficiency level, and (3) chosen by students based on their own interests. Second, we concluded that meeting individual needs requires not only matching children to texts that contain the "right" reading level. Meeting individual needs also requires a clear understanding of the reading strategies that commonly differentiate good and poor readers and deep knowledge of instructional practices that have proven successful in supporting children's acquisition and use of the strategies. We visited the classroom of Karen Murray of Nantucket, Massachusetts, to become familiar with how one teacher uses the evidence to guide her instructional decisions on a typical day.

In Chapter 6 we integrate the ideas related to each of the fundamental principles—knowing what to teach, how to teach, and when to teach—as we "walk through" a typical week in yet another second-grade classroom. The week's activities are described using the teacher's own words, written plans, photographs of classroom events and activities, and students' work samples.

Try It Out

1. Plan a literacy block that uses a variety of grouping configurations. Try to incorporate whole-class instruction, peer dyads, needs-based groups, cooperative groups, and individual learning. Compare your plan to those described in the chapter. Does your plan allow you to meet the different types of reading needs displayed by your students? Try it out and after a few days, make adjustments, until you have a routine that works well for you and your students.

2. Watch students as they engage in different kinds of groups. Observe buddy reading: Are the students reading and supporting each other? In literature circles, are students engaged in listening to each other? In what ways do they respond to each other's book talks? In cooperative groups, are all children involved in the learning? What might you do to increase children's engagement and participation in these various activities?

CHAPTER 6

A WEEK IN A SECOND-GRADE CLASSROOM

I n Chapters 1–5 we described research-based instructional practices, and we introduced you to some highly effective second-grade teachers. We gave you glimpses of effective practice by sharing these teachers' descriptions of their teaching practices and samples of their students' written work.

In this chapter our purpose is to provide an understanding of how each of these seemingly separate practices might come together in the course of a typical week in one second-grade classroom. The teacher we visit is Vickie Kagan, a second-grade teacher in Anytown, Massachusetts. Vickie has been teaching for over 20 years. The week described here took place in early December, when the school year for her second graders was well under way, and the routines were clearly established.

To frame this chapter, we present Vickie's daily and weekly schedules-at-a-glance (Figures 6.1 and 6.2), descriptions of her teaching actions, and student work samples. In addition, we share Vickie's own words as she describes and reflects on the reasons for her instructional decisions and actions.

Before you read the account of Vickie's week, we encourage you to review the evidence-based principles of best practice presented in Chapter 1. As you read, consider the relationship between Vickie's instructional routines and practices and those principles. You may wish to make a list of the ways in which Vickie's routines and practices connect to the principles of best practice, for your later use as you reflect on and plan literacy lessons in your own classroom.

Vickie's weekly schedule comprises a series of activities and events that occur every day of the week. She and the children use common labels to refer to these: opening routines, morning meeting, sustained silent reading, book talks, and clos-

Monday

8:10–8:30	Opening routines
8:30–8:50	Morning meeting
8:50–9:20	Teacher read-aloud
	Word study
9:20–9:50	Community reading
9:50–10:00	Bathroom and snack
10:00–10:20	Science and literacy
10:20–10:35	Quick penmanship review
10:35–11:00	Choral reading
11:00–11:30	Sustained silent reading
11:30–11:45	Quick book talks
11:45–12:30	Lunch
12:30–1:30	Math
1:30–2:00	Book buddies: second-grade students are partnered with fifth graders
2:00–2:20	Closing routines/ afternoon meeting

Tuesday

8:10–8:30	Morning routines
8:30–9:20	Art
9:20–9:40	Morning meeting
9:40–9:50	Teacher read-aloud
9:50–10:15	Word study
10:15–10:30	Bathroom and snack
10:30–11:30	Directions for learning centers
	Guided reading groups
11:30–11:45	Sharing
11:45–12:30	Lunch
12:30–1:30	Math
1:30–2:00	Science
2:00–2:20	Closing routines/ afternoon meeting

Wednesday

8:10–8:30	Opening routines
8:30–8:50	Morning meeting
8:50–9:15	Teacher read-aloud
9:15–9:45	Music
9:45–10:00	Snack and bathroom
10:00–10:30	Sustained silent reading
10:30–10:45	Quick book talks
10:45–11:30	Guided reading groups and learning centers
11:30–11:45	Sharing
11:45–12:30	Lunch
12:30–1:30	Math
1:30–2:00	Social studies
2:00–2:20	Closing routines/ afternoon meeting

Thursday

8:10–8:30	Opening routines
8:30–8:50	Morning meeting
8:50–9:30	Teacher read-aloud
9:30–10:00	Sustained silent reading
10:00–10:15	Student-led book talk
10:15–10:30	Bathroom and snack

cont.

FIGURE 6.1. Vickie's weekly schedule.

10:30–11:30	Guided reading groups and learning centers	9:50–10:20	Word study
			Buddy spelling test
11:30–11:45	Sharing	10:20–10:30	Bathroom and snack
11:45–12:30	Lunch	10:30–10:50	Sustained silent reading
12:30–12:50	Math		
12:50–1:30	Physical education	10:50–11:00	Quick book talks
1:30–2:00	Math	11:00–11:35	Guided reading groups and learning centers
2:00–2:20	Closing routines/ afternoon meeting		
Friday		11:35–11:45	Sharing
8:10–8:25	Opening routines	11:45–12:30	Lunch
8:25–8:55	Health	12:30–1:15	Regarding art (once a month)
8:55–9:20	Morning meeting	1:15–2:00	Math
9:20–9:50	Community reading	2:00–2:20	Closing routines/ afternoon meeting

FIGURE 6.1. *cont.*

ing routines/afternoon meeting. In presenting the portrait of a typical week, we provide a full description of these events as they occur on Monday. On subsequent days, we simply note their occurrence within the sequence of other events. In addition, there are events that occur one or more times a week. These include community reading, teacher read-aloud, learning centers, guided reading, and word study. We provide a full description of each of these on the first day that it occurs, and a brief reference to it on subsequent days.

MONDAY

Opening Routines

Each day, as students enter the classroom, they encounter Vickie standing just inside the doorway, where she greets each youngster by name and shakes hands. After hanging coats and jackets and storing backpacks and other possessions in designated locations, the children quickly attend to established early morning routines. Most students use this time to choose books for both in-class and take-home reading. The in-class books are those that they will read whenever they are

8:10–8:30	Opening routines
8:30–8:50	Morning meeting
8:50–9:15	Teacher read-aloud/community reading
9:15–9:45	Specialist—art, music, physical education
9:45–10:00	Snack and bathroom
10:00–10:30	Sustained silent reading
10:30–10:45	Quick book talks
10:45–11:30	Guided reading groups and learning centers
11:30–11:45	Sharing
11:45–12:30	Lunch
12:30–1:30	Math
1:30–2:00	Social studies or science
2:00–2:20	Closing routines/afternoon meeting

FIGURE 6.2. Vickie's daily schedule.

between learning events or during the time of day designated as sustained silent reading. The take-home books are those that the children are expected to read outside of school, either alone or with other family members.

Students may also use this time to fill out their independent reading log, recording the books they have read and rating the degree of difficulty—*easy, just right,* or *difficult.* In addition, they give a one-sentence summary or recommendation of the book and check off either "I read this book by myself" or "I listened to someone read this book." After filling out the logs, they return them to their literacy portfolios, which are filed alphabetically in a milk crate in a corner of the classroom.

Additionally, students may spend this early morning time completing learning center activities from the previous day, or they may choose to read one of their self-selected books.

Morning Meeting

After all of the children have arrived, a student leader calls them to the rug for morning meeting. (Each day, Vickie chooses two new student leaders by moving a clothespin down an alphabetical class chart.) Student leaders assume many responsibilities: They record attendance by reading and checking off each child's name from a class list; they also take lunch orders, carefully recording and tallying their classmates' menu choices. They guide their classmates in the completion of the calendar and weather charts, and they lead a choral rereading of a familiar poem or chant. Then the student leaders choose a book to read aloud to their classmates.

During the time that children attend to each of these activities, Vickie meets with individuals or small groups of students to accomplish various instructional tasks. For example, she might hold a brief student conference, chatting with a student about the previous day's take-home book or homework assignment; or she might use the few minutes available to her to take a running record of a child or two. At times, she forms "ad hoc" groups of students to address similar concerns or learning needs. Sometimes she uses the time to observe the large student-led group and to document individual or group behaviors: For example, are they on task, practicing turn taking, and getting the floor in appropriate ways?

Vickie commented to us that when she describes her morning routines to other teachers, many are skeptical and question the ability of a young second grader to assume such responsibility. However, Vickie explains that her children are well coached, and they are able to carry out these responsibilities with little or no intervention. In her own words:

> "At first, students feel nervous about being student leader, but then they love it! Some students are quiet and shy. Being student leader builds confidence as they have more turns. Parents often say, 'I don't think my child can do it!' but then they are amazed. I know they love it, because they count down on the chart and know when their turns are coming."

We have observed Vickie's classroom in action and have witnessed her children skillfully assuming leadership. We discovered that her trust in their ability to lead is well founded.

Teacher Read-Aloud

Vickie typically begins each week with a read-aloud that in some way connects various curricular areas. For this week, Vickie has chosen to read aloud a book about stars called *Stargazers* (Gibbons, 1999). She chose this book because of its connection to two areas of the curriculum. First, the school community as a whole is currently dedicated to the theme "Reach for the Stars." The expectation is that at every grade level, teachers will engage children in discussions of their personal goals and ambitions and of what it means to "reach for the stars." Second, the grade 2 science text is titled *Discover the Wonder: Earth and Sky* (Scott-Foresman, 1994), and the present focus in this year-long study is an exploration of stars.

Before she reads aloud, Vickie reviews with the students the differences between fiction and nonfiction texts. This difference has been an ongoing topic of discussion in the classroom. Most recently, she has modeled the strategy of determining the type of text in preparation for reading. Vickie displays the text she has chosen for today and asks children to predict whether it is fiction or nonfiction and to explain their predictions. After a brief discussion and affirmation of the text as a nonfiction selection, Vickie asks the children what they think they might read about in this nonfiction text. She encourages the children to share their ideas with the person next to them, and then she gives a few children a chance to share their ideas with the entire class. She reads the text aloud, stopping frequently to invite children to comment on the text and illustrations and to ask questions.

After reading, Vickie asks the children to tell the person next to them a few things they learned about stars. After just a minute or 2, she calls for volunteers to share their responses with the whole class. Then Vickie calls the children's attention to the theme baskets in which she has placed many books about the earth, sun, and stars. These baskets are labeled *fiction* and *nonfiction*. Vickie asks the children to consider which basket this particular book belongs in and why, and then asks one child to deposit the book in the appropriate basket. She reminds the students that they may choose from the books in these baskets for sustained silent reading and take-home reading or to help them as they write about stars.

Word Study

Vickie relies on two texts by Gay Su Pinnell and Irene Fountas, *Word Matters* and *Phonics Lessons,* to plan her word study lessons. This week's lessons are focused on decoding words with *r*-controlled vowels. Vickie selects the word *star* as a keyword. She discusses the vowel–*r* pattern and models the use of the strategy to read the word *star.* Then she introduces other exemplar words that will become part of the classroom Word Wall: *her, for, first,* and *fur.* Vickie elicits a list of words with the same vowel pattern from the students, and she writes these words on the chart. As the students offer words, Vickie lists them. She guides the children in reading the written words, they talk about word meanings, and they use some of them in sentences.

Next, the students select words

Fiction–nonfiction sorting baskets.

for their individual word lists. These word lists represent their spelling words for the week. To do this, students choose one word from each vowel pattern on the chart, and they add three more words from their high-frequency word list. This list was generated by assessing each student's ability to spell words from high-frequency words lists. Those words that they could not spell became part of their high frequency list. They write each of the words on their list (five *r*-controlled vowel words and three high-frequency words) on index cards. They practice their words by spelling each word using magnet letters and a strategy described as "Make, say, mix, check" (Fountas & Pinnell, 2002, p. 417).

Community Reading

Vickie uses the district-adopted basal reading program anthology for community reading. She explains that she likes the anthology because it provides her with high-quality, grade-appropriate literature selections representing both narrative and expository texts.

Vickie prepares her students to read the first selection *Do You Know about Stars?* by using the KWL strategy (Ogle, 1986). With the students seated at their desks, she gives each two Post-it Notes, one green and one yellow. She asks students to jot down a fact they think they know about stars on the green note; on the yellow note she asks them to record something they want to know or are wondering about regarding stars. As students come to the rug to start the reading, she directs them to post their notes on the KWL chart. They review their collected ideas and questions, and then Vickie directs most of the students to return to their seats to read the selection on their own. After reading, they are asked to find an interesting fact about stars and record it on a Post-it Note to share with the whole class. Vickie stays on the rug with five students who need more support to read grade-level text. Together, they chorally read the selection. Then, as a

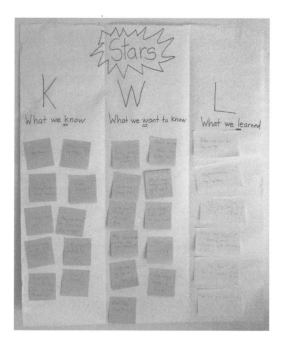

KWL chart.

group, these students recall some interesting facts about stars, and Vickie assists them in writing their ideas.

Vickie explains why she perceives community reading as an important reading routine:

> "Community reading allows us all to use a common language. It's nice. I can say to all the students, 'Remember when we all read that story?' It builds community because we are all talking about the same thing. All kids get to read the same text, some with support."

When the children who worked independently have completed reading and recording information about stars, they return to the meeting area and add their Post-it Notes to the "L" column on the KWL chart. They take a place on the rug, and Vickie asks them to share the ideas they recorded on their notes. Then she again turns the children's attention to the text, and she points out typographic cues from the selection—how the typeface changes in interesting ways: large, bold print, circular text, and large loops with the text curved to mirror the evening sky. She explains to the students that when they go to the writing center that week, they will be asked to write "shape" poems. She models a sample on the chart paper. She writes "The sun is a star," writing the word *sun* in a round shape and drawing a star around the word *star.* She encourages her students to look back at the examples in this selection to help them plan their writing. (Figure 6.3 reproduces the directions the children followed in the writing center on this day.)

Connecting Reading and Science

After a brief restroom and snack break, the students return to the meeting area on the rug. Vickie now connects her literacy lesson to a science lesson by asking the students to compare the sun to the stars. "Let's find similarities and differences," she says, and as children respond, she lists their ideas on a chart.

The students return to the KWL chart. Vickie asks, "In all of our reading so far today—in the book that I read aloud to you, in the story that you read in your anthology, and in the discussions that we have had together—what did we learn about stars? Let's add the new information to the chart." Students offer such information as "Stars look small because they're far away," and "Some stars that look smaller may be much bigger, but they're much farther away."

Choral Reading

Vickie uses choral reading to continue to develop children's understanding of the weekly theme and to support children's developing reading fluency. On this day,

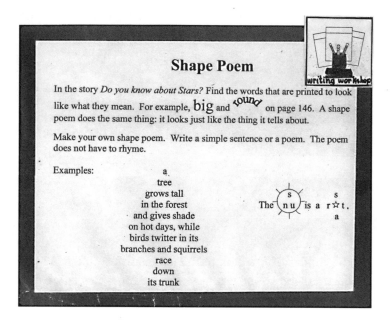

FIGURE 6.3. Shape poems.

Vickie displays five poems she has written about stars on overhead transparencies. With the children still seated together on the rug, Vickie leads her students in repeated readings of the poems. First, Vickie reads the poems aloud, pointing to each word. Next, she engages the children in "echo reading"—that is, Vickie reads each line as the students echo her words. The third reading is choral reading, with Vickie and her students reading the poems together.

Vickie then shows the students a Star Poem Booklet in which she has assembled copies of the poems they just read. Vickie tells the students that they will each get a copy of the poetry booklet, and as one of their learning center activities, they will practice reading their poems with a partner, and they will also illustrate them. (See Figure 6.4 to examine some of the poems in the Star Poetry Booklet.)

Sustained Silent Reading

Each day Vickie's students read silently from self-selected texts. Some students sit at their seats; others choose to find a comfortable spot on one of two rugs in the classroom. The students typically read for 30 minutes. Vickie does not choose or suggest books for the children to read; rather, they choose books of interest from the extensive classroom library or from home collections. However, if Vickie

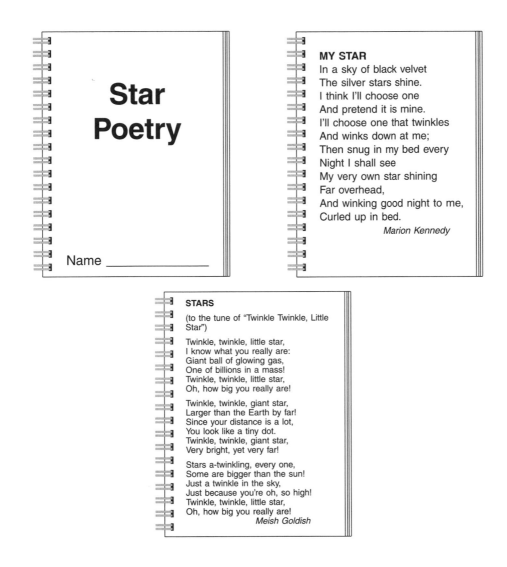

FIGURE 6.4. Star Poetry booklet.

notices that certain children consistently read books that are either too easy or too difficult for them, she gently recommends other books that might provide either greater comfort or more challenge. After sustained silent reading, the students return their books to their individual book boxes. These boxes are filled with books for sustained silent reading, take-home reading, and other occasions when the students read to learn about topics of interest.

Book Talks

"Quick book talks" typically follow sustained silent reading. The student leaders of the day share what they have read by giving the title and author and a short summary of book. Then they take comments or questions from the group. If needed, students may refer to a chart that is strategically positioned near the meeting area. The chart lists possible questions that they might ask. For example, students may ask:

"Did you have a favorite character?" "Were there any interesting words?"

"Did it remind you of something you read in another story or something that happened to you?"

These quick book talks allow the students to showcase their own reading preferences and experiences, and they often motivate other students to read the books that have been shared.

Student-developed book talk prompts.

Book Buddies

Each Monday the children meet for 15 minutes with their fifth-grade Book Buddies. Vickie and her fifth-grade colleague implemented the Book Buddies program as a way to engage second- and fifth-grade students in reading for fun and as a way to encourage students of all ages to view reading as a context for social interaction. During this time of day, the second-grade children may read a favorite text aloud, ask their fifth-grade buddy to read to them, or engage in some variation of shared reading—for example, alternating page by page or choosing to use echo reading or choral reading.

Closing Routines and Afternoon Meeting

At the end each day Vickie gathers her students into the meeting area. She uses this time to reflect on and assess the day's events by asking her students the following questions:

"What did you learn today?"

"What did you learn to help you be a better reader, writer, mathematician?"

"What did you learn about word study?" This practice helps her students understand that the day's events have been purposeful and meaningful. Vickie explains:

"This activity helps the students build community. I ask them to reflect on themselves as persons. Also, I ask them, 'Did you do something that I would be proud of?' 'Did you see someone do something nice?' 'Did you compliment someone?' 'Did someone compliment you?' It's a great way to end the school day—on a positive note."

TUESDAY

Opening Routines and Morning Meeting

As on Monday, this day begins with the opening routines and morning meeting.

Word Study

After morning routines and morning meeting, Vickie's students participate in word study activities. The students continue working with words that have *r*-controlled vowels. Vickie introduces a poem, "Mary Wore Her Red Dress," because it contains many of the *r*-controlled words that the students generated for the word list. First

End-of-day reflection prompts.

she reads the poem aloud then the students participate in a choral reading of the poem. After reading, she leads them in generating more examples of words with *r*-controlled vowels and lists these words on the chart.

Back at their seats, the students pair up with their spelling buddies to study their individual spelling lists using the "look, say, cover, write, check" sequence. Buddies are homogeneously grouped into peer dyads based on their spelling performance. In this format students look at their spelling words, say them aloud, cover them, write them on lined paper, and check them to make sure they have spelled them correctly.

Learning Center Activities

Tuesday is the first day of the week that children are assigned to learning centers. Using the work board strategy advocated by Fountas and Pinnell (1996), Vickie displays the work board and reminds students that they need to rotate through each of the assigned learning centers during the course of the morning. She reviews the directions for the activities in each learning center. During this particular week, Vickie has six learning center choices: buddy reading, browsing box, science, social studies, art, and word study. (See Appendix C for the direction cards that accompany each of the learning centers.) Since Vickie introduces only one new learning center activity each week, most of these instructions serve only as a reminder. However, the new activity receives a thorough introduction. On this particular day the new activity is a word study game in the word study center. Vickie provides a step-by-step explanation of how to play the game, using the instructional materials to demonstrate how children will carry out each step. These directions are also

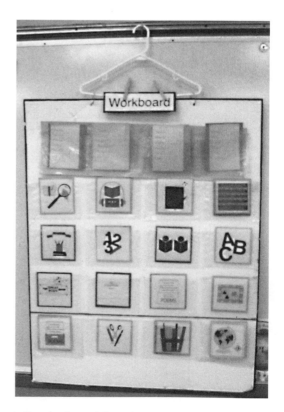

Tuesday's work board.

printed on a card that Vickie displays on a table at the word study center (Figure 6.5).

In discussing her daily routines with us, Vickie commented on the time involved in planning and preparing effective learning center activities. She explained that she does not do this by herself; rather, she collaborates with a second-grade colleague, which enables them to "share the load." In Vickie's words:

> "I am so lucky to have a great colleague who plans with me. Planning is the most difficult part of managing the classroom because there are so many activities to prepare and materials to gather. The time involved in gathering materials is a challenge. Once everything is going, it's great."

Guided Reading

Vickie works with two guided reading groups each day. She convenes one group at a time and meets with these students while the rest of the students work at the various learning centers. Although Vickie tailors instruction in each group to the needs of the particular learners, she also tends to include some guided reading routines. Among these is a presentation of a main idea statement, a picture walk, and modeling of a focal reading strategy. She provides additional support as needed, and prompts the children to use the repertoire of reading strategies that they have been learning throughout the school year.

On this day Vickie works with a group she identifies as reading at "level C," using the Fountas and Pinnell (1996) leveling system. She reviews the consonant

---

Word Study
r-controlled vowels

- Sort the word cards in the packet chart.
- Say each word. Listen to the vowel blend with *r*. Think about how the word looks and connect it with other words.
- Play the word grid game in pairs or threes.

  roll
  find
  read
  highlight (each person uses a different color)
- Take turns reading your words to group members.

FIGURE 6.5. Learning center directions: *r*-controlled vowels.

clusters with which they are still struggling, and she also reviews reading words with *r*-controlled vowels (from the earlier whole-class lesson). They use magnetic letters to make and break words, focusing on words with consonant clusters and *r*-controlled vowels. Vickie then introduces the book they will read that day: *Night Noises* by Mem Fox (1992). As students read silently, Vickie systematically observes each child in the group. When she taps a child, the child knows to "whisper read" to her. After Vickie has listened to each child read, they discuss the story as a group. Vickie explained that she tries to let the students "go where they want" in the discussion, but that she also emphasizes certain strategies. On this day she emphasizes making connections between this text and the children's personal experiences.

The second guided reading group Vickie convenes comprises children who are reading at "Level H" (using the Fountas & Pinnell [1996]) leveling system. Vickie reviews reading words containing *r*-controlled vowels, again having students use magnetic letters to form and read words. Their focal text is *The Stars: A New Way to See Them* (Rey, 1976). Vickie introduces the book and follows the same guided reading procedures as she did with the level C group.

Sharing

The students again convene as a whole class in the meeting area. One group is selected to share what they did during learning center activities. Each child in the group chooses one activity, shares it with the rest of the class, and answers questions about it.

Sustained Silent Reading, Quick Book Talks, Closing Routines, and Afternoon Meeting

To complete this day's literacy activities, children engage in sustained silent reading and quick book talks. The day concludes with the closing routines and afternoon meeting.

WEDNESDAY

Opening Routines and Morning Meeting

As on Monday, this day begins with the opening routines and morning meeting.

Teacher Read-Aloud

As she did on Monday, Vickie begins this day's literacy lessons with a read-aloud of a book about stars. This time she has selected two books; she holds up the books so that the students can see the covers, and she asks which one they would like her to read to them. Once again, she begins by focusing on the text structure. She asks the students to inspect the cover page and to study the pages as she slowly turns them. Do they think this will be fiction or nonfiction, she asks. The students agree that it will be nonfiction. She asks them to tell her how they know. After a few students respond, she affirms their prediction and reminds them to listen, as she reads, for new and interesting facts about stars. She begins to read aloud, pausing at times to invite response from the children. After reading, Vickie asks the children to tell the person next to them a new and interesting fact they learned about stars. After just a minute or two, she calls for volunteers to share their responses with the whole class. Then, as she did earlier in the week, she asks the children to consider which book basket this particular book belongs in and why, and she asks one child to deposit the book in the appropriate basket. She reminds them that they may choose from the books in these baskets for sustained silent reading and take-home reading or to help them as they write about stars.

Word Study

The children continue to practice reading words with *r*-controlled vowel patterns. Vickie reads aloud *The Emperor's Old Clothes* (Lasky, 2002). The students then look for words with *r*-controlled vowel patterns, and they add any new ones to the class chart. At their seats, the students engage in "buddy check," that is, using the magnetic letters, they spell each word and check each other's spelling. In the event of misspelled words, they highlight the word part that was difficult and make the words again with magnetic letters.

Guided Reading Groups and Learning Centers

While Vickie meets with two guided reading groups, the rest of the children consult the work board and complete the designated learning center activities.

Sharing

Children from one group share what they did at the various learning centers.

Sustained Silent Reading, Quick Book Talks, Closing Routines, and Afternoon Meeting

To complete this day's literacy activities, children engage in sustained silent reading, and quick book talks; the day concludes with the closing routines and afternoon meeting.

THURSDAY

Opening Routines and Morning Meeting

As on Monday, this day begins with the opening routines and morning meeting.

Teacher Read-Aloud

As she did on Monday and Wednesday, Vickie begins this day's literacy lessons by sharing another book about stars. She again displays two books and asks which one the children would like her to read to them. As she has done on each of the previous days, she calls their attention to the text structure and invites them to preview the cover page and browse through the pages with her. She again asks them to predict the text structure and to explain how they know. She prepares to read, reminding them to listen for interesting facts about stars. As she reads, children comment and, at times, ask questions. Because they have now read several different texts about stars, they begin making connections, pointing out that they also learned particular facts in other books. After reading, Vickie displays the books about stars that the children have read so far this week, and she asks the children to talk with the person next to them about the collection of books. Did they like one better than others? Why? Which one taught them the most? Which one had the best illustrations? After just a few minutes, she calls for volunteers to share their responses with the whole class. Once again, she asks a child to return the books to the appropriate book baskets, and she reminds the students that they may choose from the books in these baskets for sustained silent reading and take-home reading or to help them as they write about stars.

Word Study

Vickie reviews the *r*-controlled vowel word chart. The children read the words aloud, and Vickie writes the words on word cards. These word cards become part of the word wall. Students individually complete a "making connections" sheet (Pinnell & Fountas, 1998). On this sheet are three boxes: In the middle box the students write all their spelling words from the week; on one side they identify words that sound like each word on the list; on the other side they find words that look like the spelling word. (See Figure 6.6).

Guided Reading Groups and Learning Centers

While Vickie meets with two guided reading groups, the rest of the children consult the work board and complete the designated learning center activities.

Making Connections

Name: _Meaghan O'Rourke_   Date: _____

Sounds Like (These words have some of the same sounds.)	←Your Word List→ ↓	Looks Like (Other words are spelled in the same way.)
Stop jar far	Star	car stand
log Marge barge	Large	part yard
fir her girl	stir	store stare
hurled would	world	wood
church peach porch	perch	porch peach
wash wand	water	Later weather winter

FIGURE 6.6. Student work sample: Making connections.

Sharing

One group shares what they did at the various learning centers.

Sustained Silent Reading, Quick Book Talks, Closing Routines, and Afternoon Meeting

To complete this day's literacy activities, children engage in sustained silent reading and quick book talks, and the day concludes with the closing routines and afternoon meeting.

FRIDAY

Opening Routines and Morning Meeting

As on Monday, this day begins with the opening routines and morning meeting.

Community Reading

As she did on Monday, Vickie begins this day with a common text for all the children to read. This time, however, instead of using the basal reader anthology, she has selected a myth to share with children, thereby shifting their focus from the nonfiction text structure that she has emphasized throughout the week to a fictional text structure. She gathers the children on the rug in the meeting area and begins by displaying the book's cover page and reading the title, *Why the Sun and the Moon Live in the Sky*, and author, Elphinstone Dayrell (1990). She invites the children to take a picture walk with her and to predict the text structure. Do they think this text is fiction or nonfiction? Why do they think so? She encourages children to comment aloud as she turns pages, and then she tells the children that this story is a myth. She explains that throughout our history, storytellers have used myth to try to explain and understand nature. She then distributes a copy of the text to each child. Those who are capable readers are told to return to their seats, to read the story twice, and then to choose a part to read with a partner. After they finish reading, the children are asked to talk with their partner about the journal prompt that Vickie has written on the chalkboard, "Why do the sun and the moon live in the sky?," and then to record their answer in their reading journal.

Five children who need extra help remain on the rug with Vickie. They chorally read the text twice. Then Vickie turns their attention to the discussion prompt written on the chalkboard. Vickie encourages each of the children to share their ideas, and then she instructs them to record their ideas in their reading journals. She remains in the meeting area to provide help to children who need it. (See Figure 6.7 for an example of a student's written response.)

After about 5 minutes she reconvenes all of the children in the meeting area and asks volunteers to share their journal responses. Then she returns to the book and asks the children which book basket it should be placed in—fiction or nonfiction? Children respond and one child is asked to deposit the book in the appropriate basket. As she has done each day, Vickie reminds the children that this book is one they might choose for sustained silent reading or take-home reading or to help them as they write about stars.

Word Study

The whole class convenes and looks at the big chart of r-controlled vowels to which they have been adding throughout the week. Vickie asks the students to

> Why do the sun and the moon live in the sky?
>
> The sun and the Moon have lived in the sky since they had like a party with there friend water. When alot of his friends came the sun and the moon were on the roof the water friend kept coming till the roof came off. Thats how the sun and the moon came in the sky.

FIGURE 6.7. Student work samples: Why the sun and the moon?

share what was tricky for them when reading and spelling these words and to describe the strategies that helped them to remember how to read and spell the words.

Next the students have a "buddy" spelling test. Each student is tested on his or her own set of eight spelling words. To take the test, they fold a piece of paper in their notebook lengthwise. The "buddy" recites the word, uses it in a sentence, and says it again. The student writes it in his or her notebook. If the student spells it wrong, the buddy gives him or her a second chance by saying, "Try it again." After the first buddy is finished, they switch roles. If a buddy spells the word incorrectly again, this word automatically goes on the child's spelling list for the next week. Vickie explains:

> "I love this spelling procedure. It takes a lot of effort to assess and set up the individual high-frequency word lists, but it's worth it. The students really improve their spelling."

Guided Reading Groups and Learning Centers

While Vickie meets with two guided reading groups, the rest of the children consult the work board and complete the designated learning center activities.

Sharing

One group shares what they did at the various learning centers.

Sustained Silent Reading and Quick Book Talks

As on the previous four days, children engage in sustained silent reading and quick book talks.

Closing Routines and Afternoon Meeting

Although Friday's closing routines and afternoon meeting follow the same procedure as on other days, Vickie's questions become a bit more pointed and direct. Vickie explains her intent:

> "On Fridays, I want them to make deeper connections to what they learned. I want them to talk about what they learned and how they changed. I also assess myself. What did I do well this week? I can tell by listening to the students. I have certain expectations, especially on Fridays. I use this time to assess what I need to reteach the next week."

WHAT HAVE WE LEARNED FROM VICKIE?

What did you learn about Vickie and the instruction she provides for her second graders? One of the things that we know about good teaching is that there is not a single "right way" to do it. But there is much we can learn from studying the methods of a veteran teacher who has learned to put good practices together in ways that provide every child access to high-quality instruction. Vickie is one of those teachers. When we study her collected teaching actions, here is what we notice:

1. Vickie provides explicit instruction and sustained practice for her students in phonemic awareness and phonics by offering extensive and cohesive word study and learning center activities. Students are coached to say words, think about the sounds and the way the sounds correspond with letters, and then write the words. These tasks require them to develop one aspect of what Michael Graves and Susan Watts-Taffe (2002) refer to as "word consciousness"—children must use phonemic awareness to isolate individual phonemes, and they apply what they know about the letter and sound relationships to represent the sounds they hear.

2. Vickie's instruction in phonics is both contextualized—taught and practiced within meaningful and connected texts—and also decontextualized— taught and practiced as isolated word study activities. This systematic combination of activities supports the development of the word consciousness that characterizes good readers and also reinforces the essential understanding that reading is a meaning-gaining process.

3. Vickie demands that her children read a lot each and every day, and the particular activities in which she requires them to engage are especially effective in promoting reading fluency. For example, each day children have several opportunities to engage in choral and repeated readings, including the choral reading of the chart or poem during morning meeting, the rereadings of poems during learning center time, the rereading of community reading selections, and the reading or rereading of self-selected texts during sustained silent reading and take-home reading.

4. In addition to providing ample reading time, Vickie is deliberate in the types of texts her students read. During community reading, she engages every child in reading grade-appropriate text, and she makes certain that every child succeeds by using scaffolded strategies that effectively support those who are not yet able to read the text on their own. By so doing, she not only builds a community in which every child is "on the same page" (Allen, 2002) for at least part of the day—a practice that supports discussion, conversation, and camaraderie, she also increases opportunities for less-skilled readers to learn vocabulary, concepts, and language structures that are unlikely to be represented in their lower-level texts. Furthermore, she understands the importance of introducing her youngsters to both fiction and nonfiction text, and she is explicit in her discussion of text genres.

5. Vickie recognizes the importance of explicit and strategic instruction in comprehension. During virtually all literacy events, Vickie incorporates routines that remind children that the purpose of reading is to gain meaning. Teacher read-alouds, community reading, guided reading, and sustained silent reading are all characterized by opportunities for students to predict, respond, question, and share. Furthermore, Vickie does not simply assign comprehension tasks; rather, she repeatedly models and provides guided practice in comprehension strategies such as evaluating text structure, making predictions, self-questioning, making connections, and summarizing. After modeling, she uses evidence-based practices, such as KWL to help students combine and apply these strategies as they move from text to text.

6. Vickie understands that reading and writing are fundamentally social activities. In keeping with this understanding, the opportunities she presents for response and discussion are almost always collaborative in nature. During whole-class meetings, Vickie routinely pauses and invites children to share their thinking with a peer before volunteers share with the whole group. Children who read community reading selections independently join with a partner for response; after guided reading and learning center time children convene for a brief whole-class sharing time; after sustained silent reading, children convene for quick book talks. Vickie has threaded each of these activities throughout the fabric of the day, and by doing so, she impresses on children the social nature of reading and writing.

7. Vickie recognizes that meeting the full range of children's literacy needs requires multiple groups and multiple texts. During teacher read-alouds, Vickie shares texts that offer important vocabulary, concept, language, and content knowledge but may exceed the reading ability of even the most skilled readers in the classroom. During community reading, Vickie shares texts for which every child is held accountable, but without teacher scaffolding, many will not be able to read. During guided reading, Vickie carefully matches texts to children's assessed reading needs, providing opportunities for leveled skill instruction and leveled reading. During learning center activities, Vickie provides opportunities for students to practice specific skills and to engage in tasks that are known to support reading and writing fluency. By supporting sustained silent reading and take-home reading, Vickie acknowledges the importance of self-selected reading and provides yet more opportunities for students to become motivated and fluent readers.

8. For Vickie, assessment and instruction are seamlessly connected. We noticed that in her description of a typical week, she rarely made explicit reference to assessment. In fact, we found only four instances that she identified as assessment opportunities—running records that she takes as the student-led morning routines and morning meeting are underway, the running records that she takes during guided reading groups, the buddy checks that serve as spelling tests, and the afternoon routines and afternoon meeting that conclude each day. And yet, careful examination of her daily activities indicates that Vickie's students are always under her watchful eye. She watches and listens, and then she acts, placing children in guided reading groups, assigning them to particular learning centers, holding them back on the meeting area rug for help during community reading or including them in an "ad hoc" group during morning routines.

LOOKING BACKWARD AND FORWARD

In this chapter our purpose was to make the evidence-based principles that we have presented in earlier chapters "come alive" by examining the week-long practice of one highly regarded teacher. We know that teaching can be a very personal and idiosyncratic endeavor. Good teachers are distinguished not because they use the same program, or the same materials, or the same script. Rather, teachers who excel are united in their systematic attention to fundamental principles of good instruction. Our intention in providing this classroom visit is to reinforce the effective practices that are already part of your repertoire, as well as to introduce you to a few new practices that may advance you yet further down the path to excellent teaching.

In the next chapter we turn our attention to how children acquire and use literacy outside of school, and we examine the ways in which parents and teachers can work together to help children succeed in learning to read and write.

Try It Out

1. Try designing a morning or afternoon routine like Vickie's morning meeting or afternoon meeting. After a few days, reflect on the daily events. Does the new routine add an important experience to your children's literacy learning? If not, is there a way you might modify it so that it works better?

2. One of the strengths in Vickie's teaching is the way she builds on a conceptual theme throughout the children's week-long reading and writing experiences. Consider a theme that would allow you to connect children's reading and writing, social studies, and science activities. Collect books that you might use for community reading, just-right reading, and on-your-own reading. Then plan some reading and writing tasks that children could do independently at one or more of your learning centers. At the end of the week, look back over the children's work samples and reflect on what you saw and heard. Were there advantages to teaching this way? Were there disadvantages? Revise your plan and try it out again.

3. Try following your sustained silent reading time with quick book talks, like Vickie does. Begin by helping the students generate a list of questions they might use during book talk. Record their ideas on a large chart and display it in a location where the children can easily consult it. Observe them as they participate in their small groups. What do they talk about? How do respond to each other? Do they use the text to make their points? Do they connect what they read and hear to their own experiences? What might you do to help improve the book talk activity?

CHAPTER 7

DEVELOPING HOME–SCHOOL PARTNERSHIPS THAT HELP CHILDREN LEARN

I n this chapter we move beyond the confines of the classroom setting to explore the ways in which parents and teachers can work together to help children succeed in learning to read and write. The ideas we present are based on two essential claims: First, when children receive parental support in learning to read and write, they demonstrate higher levels of academic achievement (Henderson & Berla, 1994). Second, teachers can make a difference in the extent to which parents become involved in their children's learning (Edwards, Pleasants, & Franklin, 1999; Epstein, 2001; Shockley, Michalove, & Allen, 1995). As in earlier chapters, we first present the evidence that supports these claims, and then we suggest ways in which the evidence can be applied to classroom practice. Next, we examine classroom practice—but this time, rather than visit a single classroom, we visit a family literacy project. At the Intergenerational Literacy Project in Chelsea, Massachusetts, immigrant parents gather 4 days a week to learn how to advance their own English literacy and also support their children's literacy learning. We describe some of the activities that are practiced here to support home–school partnerships, and ways you might use them in your own classrooms.

WHAT WE KNOW ABOUT THE IMPORTANCE OF PARENTAL INVOLVEMENT

The belief that parents' involvement is an important contributor to children's school success is widely held and widely confirmed by a large body of investigations that represents different grade levels and a range of school communities (Henderson & Berla, 1994). In the case of literacy achievement, new studies (e.g., Taylor & Pearson, 2002; Jordan, Snow, & Porche, 2000) as well as old ones (e.g., Durkin, 1966; Clark, 1976) tell us that children who achieve high levels of reading achievement have the benefit of parental support and involvement. However, knowing and believing in the importance of parental involvement does not predict the ability of either parents or teachers to act on the evidence. Despite studies that indicate that teachers' actions are powerful predictors of parental involvement (Epstein, 1986), most teachers blame parents for what they perceive to be inadequate support. Note, for example, the commentary in a recent report by Steve Farkas, Jean Johnson, and Ann Duffett (2003), under the heading "AWOL Parents":

> Regardless of where they teach, most teachers say that they do not get the parental and administrative backing they need to do a good job. In one Public Agenda study, for example, 8 in 10 teachers said their own school had serious problems with parents who fail to hold kids accountable and parents who fail to set limits at home.
>
> Nearly all the teachers in the focus groups had a story to tell about being undermined by a parent, whether it's one who doesn't turn off the TV, one who allows extracurricular activities to take priority over academic work, or one who is outright disrespectful. Many described their interactions with parents in a "can you believe this "tone of voice." (p. 12)

Although the data presented in this survey suggest overwhelmingly negative experiences related to home–school interactions, parents and teachers achieve successful collaborations in many schools. What is it that makes the experiences and outcomes in these schools so different? There is convincing evidence that the difference can be captured in a single word: *partnership*. As Epstein (2001) explains:

> In partnership, educators, families, and community members work together to share information, guide students, solve problems, and celebrate successes. Partnerships recognize shared responsibilities of home, school, and community for children's learning and development. Students are central to successful partnerships. They are present in all three contexts, and they link members of these groups to each other. Students are actors and contributors, not bystanders or recipients, in the communications, activities, investments, decisions, and other connections that schools, families, and communities conduct to promote children's learning. (p. 4)

The emphasis that Epstein places on partnership as a characteristic of effective home–school efforts is evident in the work of many others. For example, Betty Shockley, Barbara Michalove, and JoBeth Allen (1995), whose work with families in first- and second-grade classrooms has been widely praised, explained that they were "trying to learn from parents what literacy events were important in their lives and share with them the important literacy events in their children's school" (p. 94). Similarly, Swap (1993) noted that "the partnership philosophy differs from the School-to-Home Transmission model in its emphasis on two-way communication, parental strengths, and problem solving with parents" (p. 49). What do teachers need to know and do to build effective and successful home–school partnerships? In the next section we summarize the understandings that we believe are fundamental to establishing a partnership model for home–school collaboration.

FROM RESEARCH TO PRACTICE: BUILDING EFFECTIVE HOME–SCHOOL PARTNERSHIPS

Let's begin with a few understandings about diverse families, their literacy and language knowledge and experiences, and their interest in their children's learning. First, studies by researchers such as Shirley Brice Heath (1983), Denny Taylor and Catherine Dorsey-Gaines (1988), William Teale (1986), and Concha Delgado-Gaitan (1992) tell us that although language, culture, and social class influence the ways in which parents and children use literacy outside of school, almost all linguistic, cultural, and social class groups use print in some ways in their home settings. The key for teachers is to find out how parents and children's use literacy in the context of their daily lives and then to engage in practices that join these family literacies with school literacies.

Second, although it is true that in many families, parents have few years of formal education and limited proficiency in English, there is no evidence that parents' interest in, or ability to support, their children's school success is dependent on their own level of education or their proficiency in the English language. Instead, the professional literature is replete with evidence of high interest, high expectations, and high levels of involvement by parents of diverse cultural and linguistic groups and educational levels (Baumann & Thomas, 1997; Delgado-Gaitan, 1992; Paratore, Melzi, & Krol-Sinclair, 1999; Valdés, 1996; Vazquez, Pease-Alvarez, & Shannon, 1994).

Third, parents from some cultural groups have different understandings of the role they are expected to play in their children's learning. For example, in some Latino cultures, parents believe that they are primarily responsible for children's attendance, punctuality, manners, and hygiene, and that their attention to curriculum-related matters would suggest disrespect toward the teacher (Delgado-Gaitan, 1992; Delgado-Gaitan & Trueba, 1991). As a result, unlike the typical "mainstream" parent who might convey interest by consulting the teacher about types or amount of homework, grade or class assignment, or a classroom seating arrangement (Lareau, 1989), these parents are deliberate in their avoidance of topics that they perceive to be the province of the teacher. In these cases, parents benefit from explicit explanation of what schools and teachers expect of them.

Fourth, for some families—suburban and urban—home lives are extremely complex. A parent may work more than one job, may have responsibility for both older and younger family members, and may be involved in any number of social issues—financial difficulty, chronic illness, substance abuse, marital discord, or criminal behavior. In some circumstances, seemingly beneficial parental involvement tasks can, in fact, be intrusive and disruptive. Learning how to listen to parents (Edwards et al., 1999) is a critical step in understanding what might work, or not, in attempting to develop a collaborative relationship with a particular family.

When we look across these four understandings, it becomes evident that to be successful, teachers must establish a framework for *exchanging*, rather than prescribing, information about the ways in which they can work together with teachers to support children's school success. There are many examples in which teachers have done just that. For example, Shockley et al. (1995) described how Betty Shockley, a first- grade teacher, and Barbara Michalove, a second-grade teacher, began the school year by issuing an open invitation to parents: "Please write and tell me about your child" (p. 19). They found that parents did, indeed, write back, and by doing so, gave them much information about the children's special talents and interests as well as family challenges. These teachers also made parent–child reading and talking about books the center of each day's homework assignments, encouraging children to choose books from the classroom library to bring home each day to read with their parents, and providing a home reading journal in which children and their parents recorded their response to the books they read together. In addition, these teachers made the children's family stories the centerpiece of both sharing time and writing workshop; bringing to the classroom the routine experiences of family life became an expected and daily classroom ritual.

In another example, Altheir Lazar (2004) suggests that teachers use the parent–teacher conference not only to provide information to parents about their children's school performance, but also as an opportunity to gather information from the parent about what children do at home. She recommends that teachers routinely ask two simple questions during conferences: "Can you tell me about your child?" and "How do you think I can best help your child learn?" By doing so, teachers are likely to shift the purpose of the context from one in which parents are expected to receive and comply with information provided by the teacher to one in which parents and teachers share information, and together, agree on a plan that will help children advance their learning.

Events that happen outside the classroom may also influence the quality of the partnership teachers and parents develop together. Swap (1993) encourages teachers to work with administrators to take simple actions that convey a welcoming atmosphere in the school at large. Suggestions include displaying signs that welcome visitors in the various languages represented in the community, arranging children's pictures and work samples in an entrance hallway in a way that engages parents in the life of the school, designating a place where parents can gather and talk, and explaining to secretaries how to greet and assist parents in ways that affirm that they are welcome and important in the life of the school community.

In the next section we continue our examination of the ways in which research guides practice in developing effective home–school partnerships. This classroom visit takes us to the Intergenerational Literacy Project, a program in the community of Chelsea, Massachusetts, that was founded to support the literacy development of immigrant parents and their children.

A CLASSROOM VISIT

The Intergenerational Literacy Project is situated within an urban community where the majority of children and their parents are recent immigrants to the United States. Most of the families are economically poor, and most of the adults and children in the families speak a first language other than English. Families and children represent many different cultures, but most come from countries in South and Central America, Africa, and Eastern Europe. Our work with these families has been widely published (e.g., Paratore, 2001; Paratore, Melzi, & Krol-Sinclair, 1999), and the studies that provided the foundation for these particular efforts have been reported in previous articles and books (e.g., Paratore, 2001; Paratore, Melzi, and Krol-Sinclair, 2003; & Krol-Sinclair, 1996).

In presenting these ideas here, rather than focus on specific classrooms, as we have in previous chapters, we have chosen to highlight particular practices that easily can be shaped for use in a multitude of settings. We describe three initiatives: (1) a monthly publication of a classroom newsletter, (2) the development of home literacy portfolios, and (3) a classroom storybook reading project. In each case our purpose is to describe contexts in which parents, teachers, and children exchange information about a particular topic or practice and then use that information to bridge uses of literacy at home and at school.

The Monthly Newsletter

The purpose of the monthly newsletter is to share with parents the details of classroom themes and activities and to elicit from them information about how the focal themes or activities connected to children's experiences outside of school. A typical newsletter from a second-grade classroom is shown in Figure 7.1. Notice how the various sections of the newsletter are designed to both inform and elicit information from parents. In this example, as the teacher received information from parents through classroom visits, phone calls, and written notes, she compiled notes on the information they shared and used the information to build connections as she and the children read, talked, and wrote about family customs and traditions.

We have found the newsletter to be a helpful resource in our efforts to achieve

---

Classroom Newsletter
September, 2003

What Makes Us All Special?

The first weeks of the school year are underway. The children have been learning and reading about the kinds of things families do together. Each day we talk about the ways we are all alike and the ways we are different. Two key concepts have been:

Children in the United States come from all over the world and represent many different races, ethnicities, genders, religions, and national origins.

Different families have different customs and traditions. Sharing and discussing these customs and traditions can help us to understand each other.

Books

Each day we read and discuss books that help us to explore the ways in which we are all alike and different. Some of the books we have read are:

- *A Birthday Basket for Tia*, by Pat Mora
- *Dear Juno*, by Soyung Pak
- *Grandma Francisca Remembers*, by Anne Morris
- *When Lightning Comes in a Jar*, by Patricia Polacco
- *The Quilt Story*, by Tony Johnston
- *Jingle Dancer*, by Cynthia Leitich Smith

We have extra copies of these books in our classroom library. Please borrow a copy to read with your child at home. If you know of other books about this topic that you think the class will enjoy, please let me know and I'll try to find a copy.

Writing

The children are preparing to write a book about their family traditions. When the books are completed, we will publish them and place them in our lending library for others to borrow and read.

cont.

FIGURE 7.1. Monthly newsletter.

Suggestions for Home

- Work with your child to make a list of the traditions and customs that are an important part of your family's life. Encourage your child to bring the list to school to share with teachers and classmates.
- Share special memories of family traditions and customs and encourage your child to write about and illustrate them.
- If you have photographs of family traditions and customs, share and discuss them with your child.
- Read one of the suggested books and discuss how your family traditions are similar or different from those in the story.

Coming Next

Beginning the week of October 17th, we will be studying patterns in nature and learning from the world around us. Among the books we will read are the following:

- *From Caterpillar to Butterfly*, by Deborah Haeligman
- *Around the Pond*, by Lindsay Barrett George
- *The Ugly Duckling*, by Hans Christian Andersen
- *Baby Chick*, by Aileen Fisher (a poem)
- *Those Amazing Ants*, by Petricia Brennan Demuth

We have copies of all of these books in the library. Borrow one to share with your child at home.

We want to learn from you. Have you noticed any patterns in nature in your own backyard or neighborhood? Have you and your child noticed and discussed changes in weather, or in flowers, or in trees? Please stop by, call, or write to us and tell us about them.

FIGURE 7.1. *cont.*

partnership rather than compliance. It is a useful vehicle for conveying to parents what children are studying and doing in school. By informing parents of the particular books and making them available in a home-lending library, children have common reading experiences at home and at school. In addition, the newsletter provides a way for parents to inform teachers of family routines and experiences that, when acted upon by teachers, can help connect children's school and home lives.

The Home Literacy Portfolio

Like the monthly newsletter, the home literacy portfolio represents an attempt to engage parents and teachers in reciprocal learning. It provides an opportunity for parents to share and explain home literacy practices with teachers and for teachers to share and explain school literacy practices with parents.

To accomplish this mutual exchange of information, teachers explain and demonstrate how parents might observe their children's uses of literacy at home during a parent meeting—often, for example, at the first "back-to-school" meeting for teachers and parents. Teachers remind parents that many of them already document their children's use of literacy by saving items in scrapbooks or memory boxes, and they relate this family practice to the types of records teachers keep in school. Teachers explain that parents' records of children's uses of literacy at home may add to what classroom teachers already know and, by so doing, provide teachers with useful information about how children are developing as readers and writers.

Teachers then give parents a special folder to use as a family literacy portfolio and ask them to document their children's literacy practices outside school by collecting samples of their children's literacy activities and saving them in the folder. Teachers and parents discuss the types of materials to collect. Emphasis is placed on the importance of including samples of children's written work (e.g., drawings, stories, and letters) as well as parents' own written observations. The artifacts that commonly make their way into home literacy portfolios are varied; a few examples are provided in Figures 7.2, 7.3, 7.4, and 7.5. The child who composed these samples, Brenda, had a hearing impairment that was not diagnosed until she entered kindergarten. At that point she was fitted with hearing aids, but her oral language development in Spanish and English was already substantially below that of her peers. Of interest in these samples is the focus on bilingual writing at home. Her second-grade teacher was exceptional, and she worked with Brenda's mom to support her language learning. These samples show some evidence of their collaboration. For example, in Figure 7.2 notice Brenda's spelling of singular and plural forms of nouns in English and Spanish; notice, too, that near the bottom of that page, Brenda has recorded a Spanish transcription of the English pronunciation of

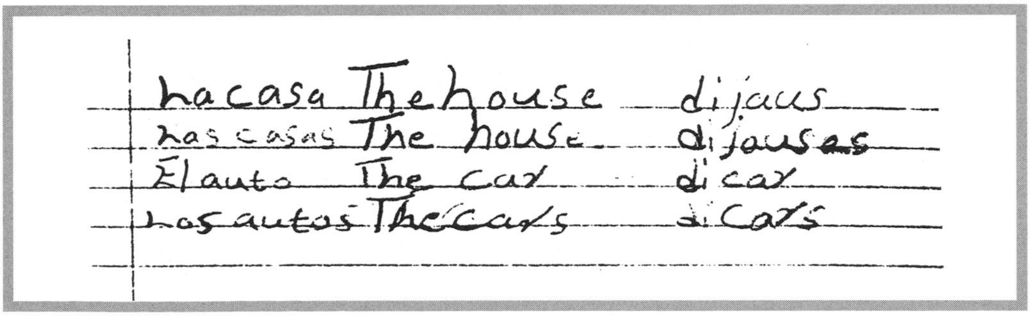

FIGURE 7.2. Child's portfolio artifact.

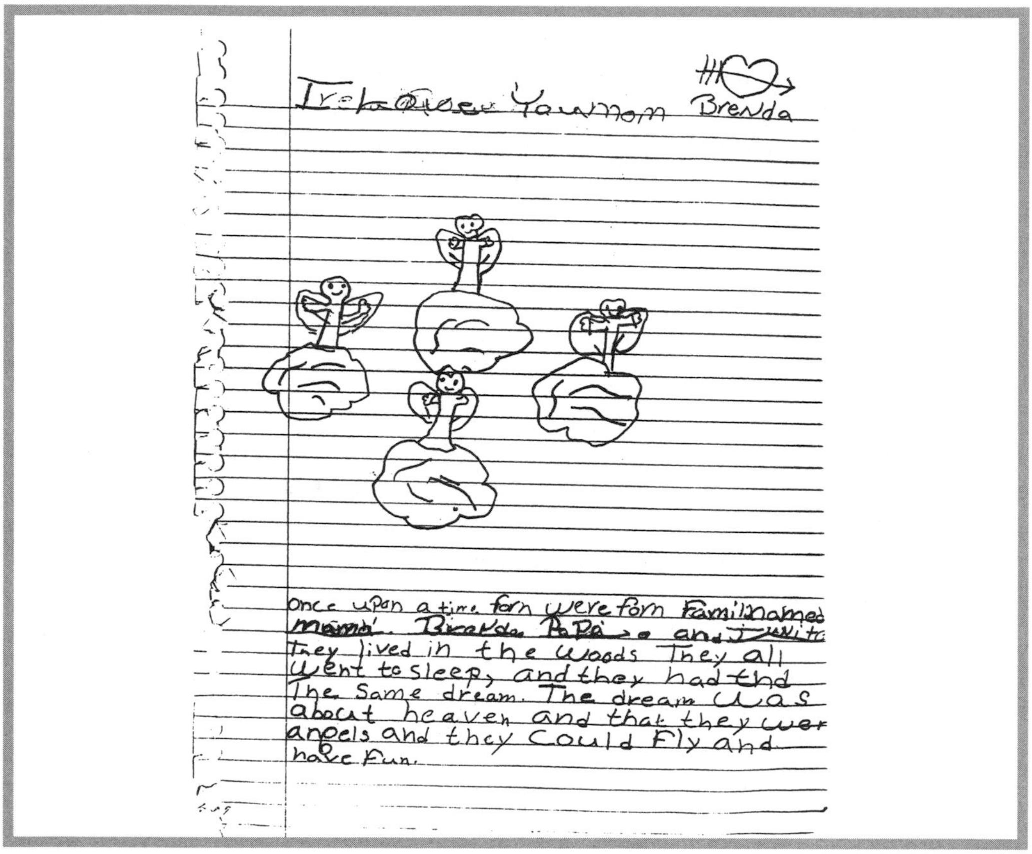

FIGURE 7.3. Child's portfolio artifact.

one of the words. In Figure 7.3 she uses English to compose a family-centered short story, and in Figures 7.4 and 7.5, she chooses Spanish to practice her recall of her religion's sacraments and commandments.

Teachers ask and encourage parents to bring the portfolios to the regularly scheduled parent–teacher conferences. During the conference, teachers provide time for parents to share the portfolios by describing each portfolio entry and the circumstances in which the child composed or completed it. Then teachers present a portfolio of children's literacy practices in the classroom. Together, parents and teachers discuss the ways in which the children's uses of literacy at home and at school connect, and they explore actions they each might take to strengthen the connections in each setting.

A number of studies has been conducted to examine the ways in which home portfolios influence the conversations that parents and teachers have during con-

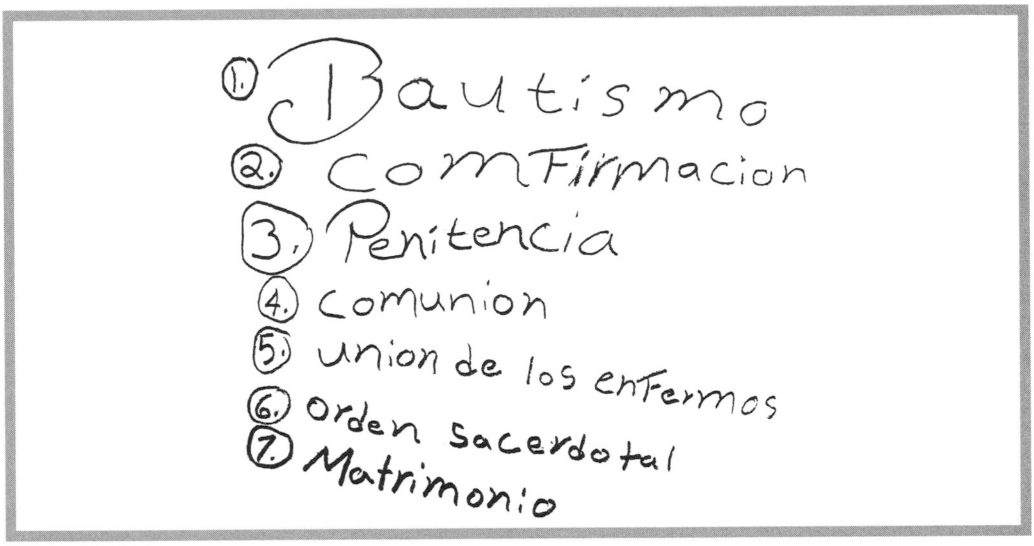

FIGURE 7.4. Child's portfolio artifact.

ferences (Paratore et al., 1995; Paratore, Hindin, Krol-Sinclair, & Durán, 1999). Evidence indicates that the use of home–school portfolios may have two especially important outcomes: (1) Teachers and parents achieve a deeper understanding of children's literacy abilities and practices; (2) learning opportunities at home and at school increase as both parents and teachers stress making connections between home and school literacy activities. If this is an initiative you would like to try with the parents of children in your classroom, the checklist presented in Figure 7.6 may help you get started.

The Parents as Classroom Storybook Readers Project

The purpose of the Parents as Classroom Storybook Readers Project is to help parents enter into partnerships with teachers by becoming skillful and frequent storybook readers. This home–school partnership project grew out of work initially developed and implemented by Krol-Sinclair (1996) and later described by Paratore et al. (2003).

Recall that the original context for this work was with parents who were new to U.S. schools, and in some cases, new English-language readers. In order to help prepare parents to become familiar with the context of the classroom and the practice of storybook reading, we began this work by providing a series of training sessions intended to introduce parents to book selection and read-aloud strategies. Although we have since exported this work to diverse school settings, we have kept the training modules as an integral part of the initiative because we have found them to be important and helpful for most parents, regardless of their educational and cultural backgrounds.

To accomplish the first step—the implementation of training sessions—someone in the school must be designated as a parent trainer. This person could be a classroom teacher, a reading specialist, a principal, or any other person who has the interest, knowledge, and time to be involved in preparing parents to become classroom storybook readers. Next, in an initial training session that may be held during or after the school day, depending on how schedules can be arranged, the parent trainer describes the classroom(s) in which parents will read, explains what a typical story-

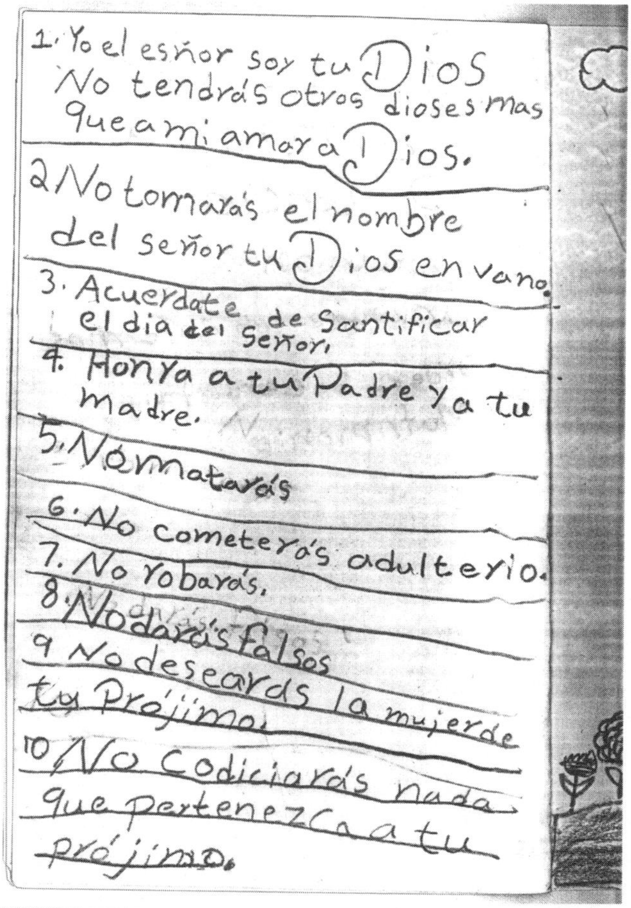
1. Yo el esñor soy tu Dios No tendrás otros dioses mas que a mi amor a Dios.
2 No tomarás el nombre del señor tu Dios en vano.
3. Acuerdate de Santificar el dia del Señor,
4. Honra a tu Padre y a tu madre.
5. No matarás
6. No cometerás adulterio.
7. No robarás,
8. No darás falsos
9 No desearás la mujer de tu Prójimo.
10 No Codiciarás nada que pertenezca a tu prójimo.

FIGURE 7.5. Child's portfolio artifact.

Family Literacy Portfolio Project
Steps to Follow

1. Invite parents to a meeting to explain the portfolio project. To accommodate the largest number of parents, try to offer two different time periods, for example, immediately before school and immediately after school.

2. At the meeting, show parents a child's school portfolio and describe the items in it. Explain that you would like to know about the kinds of reading and writing that children do at home. Provide a few examples of the types of items parents might collect or write to you about. Explain that you are most interested in the kinds of reading and writing that children do in connection with their daily routines: the books or other print materials they read for fun and recreation; the writing they do to convey messages to friends and family members.

3. Provide parents with a specially labeled folder to use to collect their home portfolio artifacts. (We give parents a brightly colored portfolio envelope that has the child's name on it.)

4. Ask parents to collect items each day and to bring the portfolio to any conference or meeting they have with you to discuss their child.

5. At the conference, invite the parent to present each portfolio piece and to tell you the circumstances that prompted the child to engage in the literacy activity. As the parent shares, when appropriate, comment on how the child's literacy practices at home connect to or extend the literacy experiences he or she has in school.

6. After the conference, consider what you have learned from the home literacy portfolio. Has it provided you with any new information about the child's understanding and uses of reading and writing? Can you make connections between the child's home and school uses of literacy?

FIGURE 7.6. Steps to follow to implement a home–school portfolio project.

book reading session is like, and models a storybook read-aloud. In the initial training session, the trainer emphasizes basic strategies, such as holding the book so that it can readily be seen by the students, stopping along the way to invite children to comment and make predictions, and encouraging children to chime in on chants and repetitive phrases. Then, following a discussion, the trainer presents parents with a selection of children's books that are appropriate for the classrooms they will visit. The trainer also summarizes the stories and highlights specific features of each book (e.g., use of rhyme or repetition). The parents are then invited to select a book to read aloud. Each parent rehearses the book one or more times, with suggestions and support offered by the trainer and the other parent participants. Before the session concludes, parents are told the date and time of their classroom storybook reading visit. These training sessions typically last 60–90 minutes.

As the next step, parents are asked to take the book home and continue to practice reading the book with their own children at home over the next few days. Then, during the next week, parents visit the designated classroom to read the selected book. When a parent enters the classroom, the classroom teacher introduces him or her to the class. Students may be seated at their desks or on a rug in a story corner. Parents read the text aloud, and, if possible, leave multiples copies of the book in the classroom for children to reread or browse through in the days that follow.

This sequence of activities is repeated each week as parents prepare new books for reading aloud; each training session emphasizes a different read-aloud strategy. Included among them are eliciting predictions before and during reading, engaging children in choral reading of chants or repetitive refrains, questioning techniques, encouraging response during and after reading, and eliciting retellings. In cases where schools house bilingual classrooms, parents may prepare to read in their first language rather than in English, to demonstrate the importance of sharing storybook reading in both first and second languages.

A study (Krol-Sinclair, 1996) of the effects of this project showed that over the course of their participation, the parents who participated acquired and used practices associated with effective storybook read-alouds when reading to children in classrooms. In addition, evidence indicated that parents used the strategies they had learned for classroom storybook reading with their own children at home, thereby improving the quality of their family reading events. Finally, although this project was specifically intended to build understanding and facility with storybook reading, parents also acquired what we might call "classroom literacy" (Corno, 1989). That is, parents who were generally unfamiliar with the learning contexts common in many U.S. classrooms—for example, cooperative learning, group discussion, open-ended response, peer interaction—had opportunities to observe such practices in action, and they came to understand that such practices do not convey disarray or lack of control; rather, they provide valuable opportunities for language and literacy learning.

The chart presented in Figure 7.7 may be useful to you in planning and implementing a Parents as Classroom Storybook Readers Project.

LOOKING BACKWARD AND FORWARD

In this chapter we set out to expand our understanding of how children acquire and use literacy by looking beyond the classroom and investigating the ways in which parents and teachers can work together to help children succeed in learn-

---

Parents as Classroom Storybook Readers

Plan a 6–8-week training module for parents to learn about effective storybook reading behaviors. Each session might include:

- An introduction to a selected book and an explanation and discussion about why it makes a good read-aloud.
- An explanation of a particular read-aloud strategy, such as stopping along the way to invite children to chime in on chants and repetitive phrases.
- A demonstration of the read-aloud, emphasizing the particular strategy (as well as behaviors such as how to hold the book so that all can see).
- Opportunities for parents to practice the read-aloud in small or large groups.
- Discussion about the classrooms in which they will read and what they should expect from the teacher and the children.

During each week, follow the same steps but add a new read-aloud strategy, and demonstrate how strategies may be combined when reading particular books. Also discuss why some strategies are more or less appropriate depending on the book.

FIGURE 7.7. Steps to follow to implement the Parents as Classroom Storybook Readers project.

ing to read and write. We set forth two claims: First, when children receive parental support in learning to read and write, they demonstrate higher levels of academic achievement; second, teachers can make a difference in the extent to which parents become involved in their children's learning. We then provided examples of strategies and practices that teachers have planned and implemented in response to these claims. Each of the examples we presented shared a common, fundamental principle: that effective home–school partnerships are built through activities and events that are based on the *exchange* of information between parents and teachers.

In the chapter that follows, we consider resources that we believe you will find helpful in creating the contexts and implementing the instructional practices that we have emphasized throughout this text.

Try It Out

■ Consider the ideas in this chapter about developing home–school partnerships. Choose one idea or activity to try with the parents of your children. Focus on an activity or two that will accomplish two purposes: to teach parents about the types of literacies you expect children to acquire and use in school, and to learn from parents about the types of literacies they use at home. (Remember that home–

school partnerships do not build quickly—they take time and persistence.) After several weeks of interacting with parents in the selected activity, reflect on the interactions. Are you noticing any changes in the ways you and the parents work together? Is there anything you might do to improve the interactions? Discuss your experiences with a teaching colleague and "pool" your ideas.

CHAPTER 8

RESOURCES AND MORE

Throughout this book, we have explained specific instructional contexts and strategies that characterize effective teaching at any grade level and, in particular, in second grade. We cited evidence (e.g., Allington & Nowak, 2004; Bond & Dykstra, 1997) to support our claim that high achievement in reading correlates not with particular programs or instructional materials but with teaching behaviors that knowledgeable and skillful teachers overlay onto an array of instructional texts or resources. Having access to excellent teaching resources makes teaching just a little bit easier; indeed, the availability of high-quality student materials may contribute to teachers' efforts to motivate and engage children in learning. In this chapter we list and describe some of the instructional resources that we believe can contribute to good teaching. This is not meant to be an exhaustive list—rather, just a few suggestions that will get you started in your quest for more information in a particular area of interest.

CLASSROOM RESOURCES FOR TEACHERS AND STUDENTS

Recall that in Chapters 1 and 3 we discussed selecting books for your second graders that matched their social, emotional, and cognitive development. We mentioned that good teachers take into account the characteristics of their students when choosing books for their classroom libraries, for their reading instruction, and for teacher read-alouds. What follows is a brief list of books for second graders that adheres to these characteristics. The books in each category represent a range of genres. We have coded each resource as easy (E), average (A), or more challenging (C). We also make suggestions for books in these categories that would make good read-alouds (RA). For example, a code of (A, RA) means that the book is of average difficulty for a second grader, and it is also suitable for a teacher read-aloud.

Families

Brown, T. (1991). *Lee Ann: The story of a Vietnamese-American girl.* New York: Cobble Hill Books. (C)

Bunting, E. (1988). *How many days to America?* New York: Clarion. (A)

Byars, B. (1996). *My brother, Ant.* New York: Viking. (C)

Heise, F. P., & Gilleland, J. H. (1990). *The day of Ahmed's secret.* New York: Scholastic. (E, RA)

Jukes, M. (1984). *Like Jake and me.* New York: Dragonfly Books. (C)

Mitchell, M. (1998). *Uncle Jed's barber shop.* New York: Alladin. (A, RA)

Williams, V. (1984). *A chair for my mother.* New York: Harper Trophy. (A, RA)

Humor

Aardema, V. (1975). *Why mosquitoes buzz in people's ears.* New York: Dial Books. (A, RA)

Allard, H. (1985). *Miss Nelson is missing.* Boston: Houghton Mifflin. (A)

Cazet, D. (1998). *Minnie and Moo go dancing.* New York: DK Ink. (C)

Hopkins, L. B. (1984). *Surprises.* New York: HarperCollins. (A)

Lester, J. (1989). *How many spots does a leopard have?* New York: Scholastic. (C, RA)

Noble, T. (1984). *The day Jimmy's boa ate the wash.* New York: Puffin Books. (A)

Fantasy

DePaola, T. (1975). *Strega Nona.* New York: Simon & Schuster. (A, RA)

DePaola, T. (1982). *Strego Nona's magic lessons.* Olando, FL: Harcourt Brace. (A, RA)

Fleishman, P. (2002). *Weslandia.* Cambridge, MA: Candlewick Press. (A)

Kimmel, E. A. (1988). *Anansi and the moss-covered rock.* New York: Scholastic. (E, RA)

Meddaugh, S. M. (1992). *Martha speaks.* Boston: Houghton Mifflin. (A).

Wolkstein, D. (1979). *White wave: A Chinese tale.* New York: Philomel Books. (A)

Zelinsky, P. (1986). *Rumplestiltskin.* New York: Dutton. (A–C, RA)

Friendship/Peer Acceptance

Henkes, K. (1988). *Chester's way.* New York: Greenwillow. (A, RA)

Lobel, A. (1970). *Frog and toad are friends.* New York: Scholastic. (E–A)

Lobel, A. (1971). *Frog and toad together.* New York: Scholastic. (E–A)

Lobel, A. (1976). *Frog and toad all year.* New York: Scholastic. (E–A)

Lobel, A. (1979). *Days with frog and toad*. New York: Scholastic. (E–A)
Marshall, J. (1982). *Fox and his friends*. New York: Dial. (A)
Rathman, P. (1991). *Ruby the copycat*. New York: Scholastic. (E, RA)
Waber, B. (1975). *Ira sleeps over*. Boston: Houghton Mifflin. (E, RA)

CROSS-CURRICULAR LINKS

In this section we recommend books that we hope will help you make cross-curricular links. To identify topics likely to be taught in second grade, we used the content standards identified in the Massachusetts State Frameworks. Our assumption is that primary-grade topics are likely to be largely similar from state to state. We provide a brief list of trade books to read and enjoy when teaching your students the contents of math, science, and social studies. Once again, we have used the same codes for the trade books as we did in the previous section. They have been coded as easy (E), average (A), more challenging (C), and suitable for a read-aloud (RA).

At the end of each content area, we make suggestions for obtaining information and gathering resources, including magazines, software, videos, and interactive websites. When choosing magazines and media for your classroom, we recommend reviewing the guidelines for selecting magazines, videos, and software in Chapter 3, which are listed in Figures 3.1, 3.2, and 3.3.

Mathematics

Trade Books

We have divided this section into five main topics that are typically associated with second-grade mathematics: number sense and operations; patterns, relations, and algebra; geometry; measurement; and data analysis, statistics, and probability.

NUMBER SENSE AND OPERATIONS

Cristaldi, K. (1996). *Even Steven and odd Todd*. New York: Scholastic. (E)
Duke, K. (1998). One guinea pig is not enough. New York: Dutton Children's Books. (A)
Geringer, L. (1987). *A three hat day*. New York: HarperCollins. (A, RA)
Gigante, P. (1999). *Each orange had eight slices*. New York: Harper Trophy. (A)
Hong, L. T. (1993). *Two of everything*. Morton Grove, IL: Whitman. (A, RA)
Johnson, S. T. *City by numbers*. New York: Puffin Books. (E, RA)
Mitsumasa, A. (1999). *Anno's magic seeds*. New York: Putnam. (E)

Olson, A. (1998). *Counting on the woods.* New York: DK Ink. (A)
Pinces, E. (1999). *One hundred hungry ants.* Boston: Houghton Mifflin. (A)
Schwartz, D. (1993). *How much is million?* New York: Harper Trophy. (C)

PATTERNS, RELATIONS, AND ALGEBRA

Aker, S. (1992). *What comes in 2's, 3's, & 4's?* New York: Alladin. (E)
Bulloch, I. (2002). *Patterns: Action magic.* Chanhassesn, MN: Two-Can. (C)
Dee, R. (1990). *Two ways to count to ten.* New York: Holt. (A, RA)
Mitsumasa, A. (1999). *Anno's mysterious multiplying jar.* New York: Putnam. (A)
Paul, A. W. (1996). *Eight hands round.* New York: Harper Trophy. (C, RA)
Polacco, P. (1993). *Keeping quilt.* Needham, MA: Silver Burdett. (A, RA)

GEOMETRY

Burns, M. (1995). *The greedy triangle.* New York: Scholastic. (A)
Burns, M. (1997). *Spaghetti and meatballs for all.* New York: Scholastic. (A–C)
Freidman, A. (1995). *A cloak for the dreamer.* New York: Scholastic. (A, RA)
Hoban, T. (2000). *Cubes, cones, cylinders, and spheres.* New York: Greenwillow. (E)
Lasky, K. (1994). *The librarian who measured the Earth.* Boston: Little, Brown. (C)
Murphy, S. (1998). *Circus shapes.* New York: Harper Trophy. (E)
Neuschwander, C. (1997). *Sir Cumference and the round table.* Watertown, MA: Charlesbridge. (C, RA)
Tompert, A. (1997). *Grandfather Tang's Story.* New York: Dragonfly. (A, RA)

MEASUREMENT

Axelrod, A. (1997). *Pigs in the pantry.* New York: Simon & Schuster. (A)
Axelrod, A. (1997). *Pigs will be pigs: Fun with math and money.* New York: Alladin. (A)
Briggs, R. (1997). *Jim and the beanstalk.* New York: Putnam. (A, RA)
Lionni, L. (1995). *Inch by inch.* New York: Harper Trophy. (A)
Myller, R. (1991). *How big is a foot?* New York: Yearling. (E)
Wells, R. (1993). *Is a blue whale the biggest thing there is?* Morton Grove, IL: Whitman. (A–C, RA)
Wells, R. (1995). *What's smaller than a pygmy shrew?* Morton Grove, IL: Whitman. (C)

DATA ANALYSIS, STATISTICS, AND PROBABILITY

Holtzman, C. (1997). *No fair!* New York: Scholastic. (E).
Mitsumasa, A. (1997). *Anno's math games.* New York: Paperstar Books. (C)
Murphy, S. (1997). *The best vacation ever.* New York: Harper Trophy. (A, RA)
Murphy, S. (1998). *Lemonade for sale.* New York: Harper Trophy. (A)
Pluckrose, H. (1995). *Sorting.* New York: Children's Press. (E)

Educational Software

Dino Numbers: dynotech.com/numbers.htm
Haley's Tables: freespace.virgin.net/steve.brown6/guinness.htm
Kids Tables and Time: ourworld.compuserve.com/homepages/RayLec/Numview. htm
The Quarter Mile Math: Race to Math Success: www.knowplay.com/children/ quarter-mile-level1.html

Videos

Videos for Mathematics: education.discovery.com/ul/videos/rainbow2.cfm#

Websites for Children

Count On: www.mathsyear2000.org/
Educational Java: www.arcytech.org/java/java.shtml
Math Forum: www.mathforum.org

Science

Tradebooks

We have divided selections related to science into five topics and accompanying subtopics: earth and space; life science; physical science; and technology and engineering.

EARTH AND SPACE: EARTH'S MATERIALS; WEATHER; THE SUN; PERIODIC PHENOMENA

Branley, F. (2001). *International Space Station*. New York: HarperCollins. (A, RA)
Branley, F. (2002). *The sun: Our nearest star*. New York: HarperCollins. (E)
Brown, M. W. (1989). *Wait till the moon is full*. New York: HarperCollins. (E–A, RA)
Cole, J. (1992). *The magic school bus lost in the solar system*. New York: Scholastic. (C, RA)
Dyson, M. (1999). *Space station science*. New York: Scholastic. (C)
Haskins, J., & Benson, K. (1991). *Space challenger: The story of Guion Bluford*. Boston: Houghton Mifflin. (C).
Miller, D. (2003). *Arctic lights, Arctic nights*. New York: Walker. (C, RA)
Simon, S. (1999). *Tornadoes*. New York: HarperCollins. (A–C)
Simon, S. (2003). *The moon*. New York: Simon & Schuster. (A–C)

LIFE SCIENCE: CHARACTERISTICS OF LIVING THINGS; LIFE CYCLE; HEREDITY; EVOLUTION AND BIODIVERSITY; LIVING THINGS AND THEIR ENVIRONMENT

Berger, M. (2004). *Spinning spiders*. New York: HarperCollins. (A)
Bernard, R. (2001). *Insects*. Washington, DC: National Geographic Society. (E–A)

Brown, R. (2001). *Ten seeds*. Knopf Books for Young Readers. (E)

Cole, H. (2003). *On the way to the beach*. New York: Greenwillow. (A, RA)

Crenson, V. (2003). *Horseshoe crabs and shorebirds: The story of a food web*. New York: Marshall Cavendish. (A)

Erlich, A. (2003). *Rachel: The story of Rachel Carson*. San Diego, CA: Harcourt. (C, RA)

Lewin, T. (2003). *Tooth and claw: Animal adventures in the wild*. New York: HarperCollins. (C)

Posada, M. (2002). *Ladybugs: Red, fiery, and bright*. Minneapolis, MN: Carolrhoda Books. (E)

Rockwell, A. (2001). *Bugs are insects*. New York: HarperCollins. (A)

Simon, S. (2003). *Eyes and ears*. New York: HarperCollins. (C)

Woodward, J. (1997). *Under the microscope: Forests*. Milwaukee, WI: Gareth–Stevens. (A)

Yolen, J. (1998). *Welcome to the ice house*. (C, RA)

PHYSICAL SCIENCES, CHEMISTRY, AND PHYSICS—OBSERVABLE PROPERTIES OF OBJECTS; STATES OF MATTER; POSITION AND MOTION OF OBJECTS

Bradley, K. B. (2001). *Pop! A book about bubbles*. New York: HarperCollins. (E)

Davies, K., & Oldfield, W. (1994). *My boat*. Milwaukee, WI: Gareth–Stevens. (E)

Pipe, J. (2002). *What does a wheel do?* Brookfiled, CT: Copper Field Books. (E–A)

TECHNOLOGY AND ENGINEERING: MATERIALS AND TOOLS; ENGINEERING DESIGN

Cole, J. (1986). *Cars and how they go*. New York: Harper Trophy. (E)

Davies, K., & Oldfield, W. (1994). *My boat*. Milwaukee, WI: Gareth–Stevens. (E)

Glass, A. (2003). *The wondrous whirligig: The Wright Brothers' first flying machine*. New York: Holiday House. (A, RA)

Maze, S. (1997). *I want to be an engineer*. San Diego, CA: Harcourt. (C)

Mellett, P. (1998). *Flight*. Milwaukee, WI: Gareth–Stevens. (A)

Platt, R. (2003) *Eureka! Great Inventions and how they happened*. London: Kingfisher. (C, RA)

Williams, J. (1992). *Projects with flight*. Milwaukee, WI: Gareth–Stevens. (A)

Children's Magazines

Click Magazine: www.clickmag.com

Kids Discover Magazine: www.kidsdiscover.com

Owl Magazine: www.owlkids.com

Ranger Rick Magazine: www.nwf.org/kidspubs/rangerrick/

Zoobooks: www.zoobooks.com

Educational Software

Escape from Braindeath: Virtual Physics: www.virtualphysics.com/vp1/VP1Front.html

Sidewalk Science: Bugs; *Sidewalk Science: Dirt*; *Sidewalk Science: Wheels*: www.tomsnyder.com/products/product.asp?SKU=SIDSID&Subject=Science

Sticky Bear Science Fair: www.knowplay.com/children/science.html

Videos

Videos for Science: education.discovery.com/ul/videos/rainbow2.cfm#

Websites for Children

Annenberg/CPB: www.learner.org/students

Cool Science for Curious Kids: www.hhmi.org/coolscience/

Cyber Zoomobile: www.primenet.com/~brendel/

Earth and Sky: earthsky.com/

Scientists in the City: sln.fi.edu/city/city.html

Ultra-Efficient Engine Technology Kids' Page: www.ueet.nasa.gov/StudentSite/

Social Studies

Again using the Massachusetts State Frameworks as a guide, we selected resources to support children's study of history, geography, civics, government, and economics through studies of family and family history; and resources to expand their knowledge of economics by studying consumers, producers, and buyers.

Trade Books

Adler, D., (2001). *A picture book of Sacagawea*. New York: Holiday House. (A, RA)

Barron, T. A. (2000). *Where is grandpa?* New York: Philomel Books. (A)

DePaola, T. (2002). *On my way*. New York: Putnam. (A, RA)

Kalman, M. (1999). *Next stop Grand Central*. New York: Putnam. (E)

Katz, K. (1999). *The color of us*. New York: Holt. (E)

Lin, G. (2001). *Dim sum for everyone*. New York: Knopf Books. (E)

Lin, G. (2001). *The ugly vegetables*. Watertown, MA: Charlesbridge. (E)

Miller, W. *Rent party jazz*. New York: Lee & Low Books. (A–C, RA)

Monk, I. (1998). *Hope*. Minneapolis, MN: Carolrhoda Books. (A)

Peacock, C. A. (2000). *Mommy far, mommy near*. Morton Grove, IL: Whitman. (A)

Simon, N. (1999). *All kinds of children*. Fremont, CA: Shen's Books. (E)

Children's Magazines and accompanying websites.

Calliope Magazine: Exploring World History: www.cobblestonepub.com/pages/callmain.htm

National Geographic World: www.nationalgeographic.com/world/

Educational Software

Community Construction Kit: www.tomsnyder.com/products/product.asp?SKU=CCKCCK&Subject=SocialStudies

Neighborhood Map Machine: www.tomsnyder.com/products/products.asp?Subject=
 SocialStudies

Videos

education.discovery.com/ul/videos/rainbow2.cfm#

Websites for Children

Annenberg/CPB: www.learner.org/students/
National Geographic for Kids: www.nationalgeographic.com/world/

RESOURCES FOR PROFESSIONAL DEVELOPMENT

We know that effective teachers are involved in ongoing professional development. Some of these professional development opportunities include inservice workshops, seminars, and study groups. However, we also know that excellent teachers do a great deal of professional development on their own through self-study. In the sections that follow, we provide professional resources that address selecting books for classrooms and general issues in teaching reading and writing, and we then present lists of resources that focus on particular topics. In each case we selected resources because the ideas within them are consistent with evidence-based instruction.

We begin with professional organizations because they provide many of the tools that you need to support your own professional development: They suggest books for professional development and provide extensive lists of trade books to use in the classroom, which link the content area to literacy. Many organizations provide opportunities for members to contribute to discussion boards and forums. Their websites also have many similar features: topics and issues, information about membership, publications and journals, online resources, events, outreach, and information about regional and national conferences. We suggest that you visit these sites, "bookmark" them as your "favorites," and refer to them whenever you have questions about making curriculum connections.

American Library Association: www.ala.org
The International Reading Association: www.reading.org
National Council for the Social Studies: www.ncss.org
National Council of Teachers of English: www.ncte.org
National Council of Teachers of Mathematics: www.nctm.org
National Science Teachers Association: www.nsta.org

RESOURCES FOR SELECTING BOOKS FOR YOUR CLASSROOM

Throughout this text we have emphasized the importance of selecting high-quality books for your classroom library, read-alouds, and instruction. Fortunately, teachers can get a lot of help doing this; there are many resources for selecting high-quality books for your classroom. The professional organizations listed in the previous section all provide links to recommended books. We suggest you refer to those websites, because they are updated frequently, particularly with the addition of notable books for each year. The lists are accompanied by annotated bibliographies.

Children's librarians at public libraries and your own school librarian can also be invaluable resources for choosing books for you classroom. In addition to recommending the books they have on the shelves, they often have many reference materials that can help you select suitable books for your classroom to accompany your content-area curriculum, to stock your classroom library, and for teacher read-alouds. These libraries generally have the comprehensive reference texts such as *A–Zoo: Subject Access to Picture Books* (Lima & Lima, 2001) and *Best Books for Children* (Gillespie, 2001), which list thousands of titles of books for children. These books are costly and must be updated frequently, so they are not among the books we would suggest for classroom teachers. Instead, we have listed (below) a sample of the many additional resources you can use to learn about selecting literature for your classroom. These books and resources are more affordable, and most of them give suggestions for *using* the literature as well as selecting it.

Books

Cullinan, B., & Galda, L. (2002). *Literature and the child* (5th ed.). New York: Wadsworth.

Fountas, I. C., & Pinnell, G. S. (1999). *Matching books to readers: Using leveled books in guided reading.* Portsmouth, NH: Heinemann.

Harris, V. J. (1997). *Using multiethnic literature in the K–8 classroom.* Norwood, MA: Christopher–Gordon.

Huck, C. S., Hepler, S., Hickman, J., & Kiefer, B. Z. (2001). *Children's literature in the elementary school* (7th ed.). Boston: McGraw-Hill.

Norton, D. E. (2003). *Through the eyes of a child: An introduction to children's literature.* Upper Saddle River, NJ: Merrill/Prentice Hall.

Reutzel, D. R., & Fawson, P. C. (2002). *Your classroom library: New ways to give it more teaching power.* New York: Scholastic.

Sloan, G. (2003). *Give them poetry! A guide to sharing poetry with children K–8.* New York: Teachers College Press.

Temple, C., Martinez, M., Yokota, J., & Naylor, A. (2001). *Children's books in children's hands: An introduction to their literature.* Boston: Allyn & Bacon.

Websites

100 Best Books for Kids: www.teachersfirst.com/100books.htm
Children's Literature Web Guide: www.ucalgary.ca/~dkbrown/index.html
The Horn Book, Inc.: www.hbook.com
Wonderful World of Books (ages 3–8): hometown.aol.com/rbnspn/primarybooklist. html

RESOURCES FOR INSTRUCTION

We know that there is more to implementing an effective literacy program than selecting books and other resources for your classroom, and we have tried to share with you a number of evidence-based ideas throughout this text. However, there are many more ideas available to you. This section suggests professional teaching tools that can give you great ideas for teaching your students.

Creating Effective Contexts for Literacy Learning

Kriete, R., & Betchel, L. (2002). *The morning meeting book.* Greenfield, MA: Northeast Foundation for Children.

Morrow, L. M. (2000). *Literacy development in the early years* (4th ed.). Boston: Allyn & Bacon.

Morrow, L. M. (2002). *The literacy center: Contexts for reading and writing* (2nd ed.). York, ME: Stenhouse.

Strickland, D. S., & Morrow, L. M. (2000). *Beginning reading and writing.* New York: Teachers College Press.

Teaching Word Study

Bear, D. R., Invernizzi, M., Templeton, S. R., & Johnston, F. (2003). *Words their way: Word study for phonics, vocabulary, and spelling instruction* (3rd ed.). Upper Saddle River, NJ: Prentice Hall.

Cunningham, P. M. (2005). *Phonics they use: Words for reading and writing.* Boston: Allyn & Bacon.

Ericson, L., & Juliebo, M. F. (1998). *The phonological awareness handbook for kindergarten and primary teachers.* Newark, DE: International Reading Association.

Ganske, K. (2000). *Word journeys: Assessment-guided phonics, spelling, and vocabulary instruction.* New York: Guilford Press.

Johns, J. L., & Berglund, R. L. (2002). *Fluency: Evidence-based strategies*. Dubuque, IA: Kendall–Hunt.

Opitz, M., & Rasinski, T. (1998). *Good bye round robin*. Portsmouth, NH: Heinemann.

Pinnell, G. S., & Fountas, I. C. (1998). *Word matters: Teaching phonics and spelling in the reading/writing classroom*. Portsmouth, NH: Heinemann.

Rasinski, T. (2003). *The fluent reader: Oral reading strategies for building word recognition, fluency, and comprehension*. New York: Scholastic.

Rosencrans, G. (1998). *The spelling book: Teaching children how to spell, not what to spell*. Newark, DE: International Reading Association.

Teaching Vocabulary

Baumann, J. F., & Kame'enui, E. J. (2003). *Teaching vocabulary: Research to practice*. New York: Guilford Press.

Beck, I. L., McKeown, M. C., & Kucan, L. (2002). *Bringing words to life: Robust vocabulary instruction*. New York: Guilford Press.

Blachowicz, C., & Fisher, P. J. (2002). *Teaching vocabulary in all classrooms*. Upper Saddle River, NJ: Pearson.

Pittelman, S. D., Heimlich, J. E., Berglund, R. L., & French, M. (1991). *Semantic feature analysis*. Newark, DE: International Reading Association.

Grouping Children for Literacy Instruction

Caldwell, J., & Ford, M. (2002). *Where have all the bluebirds gone?* Portsmouth, NH: Heinemann.

Opitz, M. F., & Ford, M. P. (2001). *Reaching readers: Flexible and innovative strategies for guided reading*. Portsmouth, NH: Heinemann.

Parkes, B. (2000). *Read it again! Revisiting shared reading*. York, ME: Stenhouse.

Pinnell, G. S., & Fountas, I. C. (1996). *Guided reading: Good first teaching for all children*. Portsmouth, NH: Heinemann.

Radencich, M. C., & McKay, L. J. (1995). *Flexible grouping for literacy in the elementary grades*. Needham, MA: Allyn & Bacon.

Tyner, B. (2004). *Small-group reading instruction: A differentiated teaching model for beginning and struggling readers*. Newark, DE: International Reading Association.

Teaching Reading Comprehension

Blachowicz, C., & Ogle, D. (2001). *Reading comprehension: Strategies for independent learners*. New York: Guilford Press.

Duffy, G. G. (2003). *Explaining reading: A resource for teaching concepts, skills, and strategies*. New York: Guilford Press.

Hancock, J. (Ed.). (1999). *The explicit teaching of reading*. Newark, DE: International Reading Association.

Harvey, S., & Goudvis, A. (2000). *Strategies that work: Teaching comprehension to enhance understanding*. York, ME: Stenhouse.

Hoyt, L., Mooney, M. M., & Parkes, B. (2003). *Exploring informational texts: From theory to practice*. Portsmouth, NH: Heinemann.

Keene, E. O., & Zimmermann, S. (1997). *Mosaic of thought: Teaching comprehension in a reader's workshop*. Portsmouth, NH: Heinemann.

McLauglin, M. (2003). *Guided comprehension in the primary grades*. Newark, DE: International Reading Association.

Assessing Your Students

Clay, M. M. (2002). *An observation survey of early literacy achievement* (2nd ed.). Portsmouth, NH: Heinemann.

Clay, M. M. (2000). *Running records for classroom teachers*. Portsmouth, NH: Heinemann.

Johnston, P. (2000). *Running records: A self-tutoring guide*. Portland, ME: Stenhouse.

Leslie, L., & Caldwell, J. (2000). *Qualitative reading inventory* (3rd ed.). Boston: Allyn & Bacon.

Rhodes, L. K. (1993). *Literacy assessment: A handbook of instruments*. Portsmouth, NH: Heinemann.

Developing Home–School Partnerships

Edwards, P. A., Pleasants, H. M., & Franklin, S. H. (1999). *A path to follow: Learning to listen to parents*. Portsmouth, NH: Heinemann.

Paratore, J. R. (2001). *Opening doors, opening opportunities: Family literacy in an urban community*. Needham Heights, MA: Allyn & Bacon.

Shockley, B., Michalove, B., & Allen, J. (1995). *Engaging families: Connecting home and school literacy communities*. Portsmouth, NH: Heinemann.

Thomas, A., Fazio, L., & Stiefelmeyer, B. L. (1999). *Families at school: A guide for educators*. Newark, DE: International Reading Association.

Vopat, J. (1993). *The parent project: A workshop approach to parent involvement*. York, ME: Stenhouse.

Of General Interest to Teachers of Primary-Grade Reading and Writing

Allington, R. L. (2001). *What really matters for struggling readers: Designing research-based programs*. New York: Longman.

Lazar, A. M. (2004). *Learning to be literacy teachers in urban schools: Stories of growth and change*. Newark, DE: International Reading Association.

Routman, R. (1996). *Literacy at the crossroads*. Portsmouth, NH: Heinemann.

Routman, R. (2002). *Reading essentials: The specifics you need to teach reading well*. Portsmouth, NH: Heinemann.

Readers' Theatre Scripts

www.aaronshep.com/rt/
www.42explore.com/skits&plays.htm
www.teachingheart.net/readerstheater.htm

Sample Lesson Plans for Teaching Reading and Writing

ReadWriteThink (RWT): www.readwritethink.org
Teaching Reading K–2: A Videotaped Classroom Library: learner.org/
Teaching Reading K–2: A Videotaped Workshop Series: learner.org/

PRIMARY LITERACY STANDARDS FOR SECOND GRADE

From New Standards Primary Literacy Committee (1999, pp. 144, 146, 150, 152, 154–156). Copyright 1996 by the National Center on Education and the Economy and the University of Pittsburgh. Reprinted by permission.

Second-Grade
Reading Standard 1: **Print-Sound Code**

By the end of second grade, students should have a firm grasp of the print-sound code and be able to read the full range of English spelling patterns.

By the end of the year, we expect second-grade students to:

◆ read regularly spelled one- and two-syllable words automatically; and

◆ recognize or figure out most irregularly spelled words and such spelling patterns as diphthongs,* special vowel spellings and common word endings.

*A diphthong is a vowel sound that changes as it is spoken. In the word *boy*, for example, the *oy* sounds almost as if it were two sounds, /o/ and /e/. Other examples of diphthongs include the /ay/ sound in *day* or the /ow/ sound in *cow*.

Second-Grade
Reading Standard 2: Getting the Meaning

Accuracy

By the end of the year, we expect second-grade students to be able to:

◆ independently read aloud unfamiliar Level L books with 90 percent or better accuracy of word recognition (self-correction allowed).

Fluency

By the end of the year, we expect second-grade students to be able to:

◆ independently read aloud from unfamiliar Level L books that they have previewed silently on their own, using intonation, pauses and emphasis that signal the meaning of the text; and

◆ use the cues of punctuation — including commas, periods, question marks and quotation marks — to guide them in getting meaning and fluently reading aloud.

**Second-Grade
Reading Standard 1:**
Print-Sound Code

**Second-Grade
Reading Standard 2:**
Getting the Meaning

◆ Accuracy

◆ Fluency

◆ Self-Monitoring and
  Self-Correcting Strategies

◆ Comprehension

**Second-Grade
Reading Standard 3:**
Reading Habits

◆ Independent and
  Assisted Reading

◆ Being Read To

◆ Discussing Books

◆ Vocabulary

**Leveled Books to
Read for Accuracy
and Fluency**

Level L books are markedly different from texts at lower levels. These books typically are longer chapter books with only a few illustrations that provide much less support for readers. The text size is smaller, and the word spacing is narrower.

Level L books feature more characters who are involved in more complex plots. The language structures are more sophisticated, detailed and descriptive. The vocabulary is challenging.

In general, Level L books require higher-level conceptual thinking for students to understand the subtleties of plot and character development. Students must sustain their reading over several days to finish the book. Most of the reading is done silently and independently, but some parts of the book may be read aloud for emphasis or interest. Group discussion may support readers during and after they read Level L books.

Self-Monitoring and Self-Correcting Strategies

At second grade, self-monitoring should be a well-established habit, and all the strategies developed earlier should be used regularly and almost automatically. In addition, second graders' strategies should be more focused than before on comprehension and meaning of extended sequences of text. Readers' fluency continues to drop when harder texts require them to monitor overtly for accuracy and sense and to use strategies for solving reading problems and self-correcting.

By the end of the year, we expect second-grade students to:

◆ know when they don't understand a paragraph and search for clarification clues within the text; and

◆ examine the relationship between earlier and later parts of a text and figure out how they make sense together.

Second-Grade Reading Standard 1: *Print-Sound Code*

Second-Grade Reading Standard 2: *Getting the Meaning*

◆ Accuracy

◆ Fluency

◆ Self-Monitoring and Self-Correcting Strategies

◆ Comprehension

Second-Grade Reading Standard 3: *Reading Habits*

◆ Independent and Assisted Reading

◆ Being Read To

◆ Discussing Books

◆ Vocabulary

Self-Monitoring

When students become adept at using self-monitoring strategies, their self-monitoring behaviors become less visible. Asking children to talk about the strategies they are using is a way to make self-monitoring more overt. However, children who have been taught specific ways to solve reading problems sometimes learn to talk about the methods without being able to actually apply them. It is, therefore, important to notice whether what students say they are doing matches what they do.

Comprehension

By the end of second grade, we expect children to demonstrate their comprehension of a variety of narrative, literary, functional and informational texts that they read independently or with a partner, as well as texts that adults read to them.

For books that they read independently, including functional and informational texts, we expect children at the end of second grade to be able to do all of the things we expected of them in first grade, both orally and in writing. In addition, we expect them to:

◆ recognize and be able to talk about organizing structures;

◆ combine information from two different parts of the text;

◆ infer cause-and-effect relationships that are not stated explicitly;

◆ compare the observations of the author to their own observations when reading nonfiction texts; and

◆ discuss how, why and what-if questions about nonfiction texts.

The texts that adults read to second graders usually have more complex conceptual and syntactic features than the texts the children read independently, and this permits greater depth in the kinds of comprehension children can display. For texts that are read to them, we expect children at the end of second grade to be able to do all of the things they can do for independently read texts. In addition, we expect them to:

◆ discuss or write about the themes of a book — what the "messages" of the book might be;

◆ trace characters and plots across multiple episodes, perhaps ones that are read on several successive days; and

◆ relate later parts of a story to earlier parts, in terms of themes, cause and effect, etc.

Second-Grade
Reading Standard 3: **Reading Habits**

Children in second grade read more complex books that are considerably longer than books read in first grade and that often have chapters. Because of the length and complexity of these texts, second graders often do not reread whole books in a single day. They must continue to read a lot — a longer book or several chapters per day — not only for the purpose of learning to read, but also for the sheer enjoyment of reading. They also should be reading to learn throughout the school day in all areas of the curriculum. Most of their reading should be done indepen-

> **Second-Grade
> Reading Standard 1:**
> *Print-Sound Code*
>
> **Second-Grade
> Reading Standard 2:**
> *Getting the Meaning*
>
> ◆ Accuracy
>
> ◆ Fluency
>
> ◆ Self-Monitoring and
>   Self-Correcting Strategies
>
> ◆ Comprehension
>
> **Second-Grade
> Reading Standard 3:**
> *Reading Habits*
>
> ◆ Independent and
>   Assisted Reading
>
> ◆ Being Read To
>
> ◆ Discussing Books
>
> ◆ Vocabulary

dently or with assistance from a peer partner. Nonetheless, every day, students should have read to them worthwhile literature beyond their own reading range. Such books should show the language and craft of good writing. This develops vocabulary, more complex syntax and conceptual structure, new ideas, and author's craft.

Books second-grade students read or have read to them should cross a range of genres. It is especially important that they read all the genres they are writing (see Writing Standard 2: Writing Purposes and Resulting Genres). Knowledge of genres is needed to be a good reader and writer. Each genre carries expectations shared by the writer and the reader. Each genre has its typical patterns of organizational structure. Once students understand the characteristics of a genre, reading and writing in the genre become much easier.

By second grade, students should recognize and be able to discuss literary qualities of the children's literature they read. They should identify and talk (or write) about similarities in different books by the same author; differences in similar books by different authors; genre features; and the effects of author's craft, including word choice, plot, beginnings, endings and character development.

Independent and Assisted Reading

We expect second-grade students to:

◆ read one or two short books or long chapters every day and discuss what they read with another student or a group;

◆ read good children's literature every day;

◆ read multiple books by the same author and be able to discuss differences and similarities among these books;

◆ reread some favorite books or parts of longer books, gaining deeper comprehension and knowledge of author's craft;

◆ read narrative accounts, responses to literature (pieces written by other students, book blurbs and reviews), informational writing, reports, narrative procedures, recountings, memoirs, poetry, plays and other genres;

◆ read their own writing and the writing of their classmates, including pieces compiled in class books or placed on public display;

◆ read the functional and instructional messages they see in the classroom environment (for example, announcements, labels, instructions, menus and invitations) and some of those encountered outside school; and

◆ voluntarily read to each other, signaling their sense of themselves as readers.

Being Read To

In second grade, we expect all students, every day, to:

◆ have worthwhile literature read to them to model the language and craft of good writing; and

◆ listen to and discuss at least one text that is longer and more difficult than what they can read independently or with assistance.

Additionally, we expect students to:

◆ hear texts read aloud from a variety of genres; and

◆ use reading strategies explicitly modeled by adults in read-alouds and assisted reading.

What Books Should Second Graders Read?

Beyond leveled books, which are used for practice-reading, teaching, and testing for accuracy and fluency, second graders should read a variety of books and other print material.

Many excellent fiction and non-fiction books do not appear on any leveled text lists. Classroom libraries should include a wide range of classic and modern books that will satisfy readers with various reading abilities and interests. Second graders need books at their own reading levels to practice new skills and books above their reading levels to stretch and challenge them.

Second-grade classrooms also should include books that teachers can read aloud to the students. Most second graders will not be able to read the read-aloud books on their own, but they can understand and enjoy more advanced books — and they need to hear these books read aloud to learn new vocabulary and more sophisticated syntax.

There are many lists of recommended titles, including the Newbury and Caldecott Award winners, *The Read-Aloud Handbook* by Jim Trelease, *Books to Build on: A Grade-by-Grade Resource Guide for Parents and Teachers (Core Knowledge Series)* by E.D. Hirsch, and the *Elementary School Library Collection: A Guide to Books and Other Media*. The American Library Association also recommends titles.

Discussing Books

By second grade, children should discuss books daily in peer groups as well as in teacher-led groups. Their discussions are more extended and elaborate than earlier, and students are likely to challenge and argue with one another.

In classroom discussions of their reading, we expect students finishing second grade to be able to:

◆ demonstrate the skills we look for in the comprehension component of Reading Standard 2: Getting the Meaning;

◆ recognize genre features and compare works by different authors in the same genre;

◆ discuss recurring themes across works;

◆ paraphrase or summarize what another speaker has said and check whether the original speaker accepts the paraphrase;

◆ sometimes challenge another speaker on whether facts are accurate, including reference to the text;

◆ sometimes challenge another speaker on logic or inference;

◆ ask other speakers to provide supporting information or details; and

◆ politely correct someone who paraphrases or interprets their ideas incorrectly (for example, "That's not what I meant ... ").

Second-Grade Reading Standard 1: *Print-Sound Code*

Second-Grade Reading Standard 2: *Getting the Meaning*

  ◆ Accuracy

  ◆ Fluency

  ◆ Self-Monitoring and Self-Correcting Strategies

  ◆ Comprehension

Second-Grade Reading Standard 3: *Reading Habits*

  ◆ Independent and Assisted Reading

  ◆ Being Read To

  ◆ Discussing Books

  ◆ Vocabulary

Vocabulary

We expect second-grade students to:

◆ recognize when they don't know what a word means and use a variety of strategies for making sense of how it is used in the passage they are reading;

◆ talk about the meaning of some new words encountered in reading after they have finished reading and discussing a text;

◆ notice and show interest in understanding unfamiliar words in texts that are read to them;

◆ know how to talk about what nouns mean in terms of function (for example, "An apple is something you eat"), features (for example "Some apples are red") and category (for example, "An apple is a kind of fruit"); and

◆ learn new words every day from their reading and talk.

LIST OF COMMON PHONOGRAMS

ab: tab, drab
ace: race, place
ack: lack, track
act: fact, pact
ad: bad, glad
ade: made, shade
aft: raft, craft
ag: bag, shag
age: page, stage
aid: maid, braid
ail: mail, snail
air: hair, stair
ain: rain, train
ait: bait, trait
ake: take, brake
alk: talk, chalk
all: ball, squall
am: ham, swam
arne: name, blame
amp: camp, clamp
an: man, span
ance: dance, glance
and: land, gland
ane: plane, cane
ang: bang, sprang
ank: bank, plank
ant: pant, chant
ap: nap, snap
ape: tape, drape
ar: car, star
ard: hard, card
are: care, glare

arn: barn, yarn
arp: carp, harp
art: part, start
ase: base, case
ash: cash, flash
ask: mask, task
ass: lass, mass
at: fat, scat
atch: hatch, catch
ate: gate, plate
aught: caught, taught
ave: gave, shave
aw: saw, draw
awn: lawn, fawn
ay: hay, clay
ax: wax,sax
aze: haze, maze
ead: head, bread
eak: leak, sneak
eal: real, squeal
earn: team, stream
ean: mean, lean
eap: heap,leap
ear: year, spear
eat: beat, cheat
eck: peck, check
ed: bed, shed
ee: tee, tee
eed: need, speed
eek: leek, seek
eel: feel, kneel
eern: deem, seem

eer: beer, peer
eet: feet, sleet
eg: leg, bet
eigh: weigh, sleigh
eight: weight, freight
ell: fell, swell
elt: felt, belt
en: Ben, when
end: tend, send
ent: sent, spent
ess: less, bless
est: rest, chest
et: get, jet
ew: flew, chew
ib: bib, crib
ibe: bribe, tribe
ice: rice, splice
ick: kick, stick
id: hid, slid
ide: wide, pride
ie: die, pie
ief: thief, chief
ife: wife, knife
iff: cliff, whiff
ift: gift, sift
ig: pig, twig
ight: tight, bright
ike: Mike, spike
ile: mile, tile
ill: fill, chill
ilt: kilt, quilt
im: him, trim

From Rasinski and Padak (2001, pp. 217–218). Copyright 2001 by Addison-Wesley Educational Publishers, Inc. Reprinted by permission.

ark: dark, spark
arm: harm, charm
ind: kind, blind
ine: mine, spine
ing: sing, string
ink: sink, shrink
ip: hip, flip
ipe: ripe, swipe
ire: tire, sire
irt: dirt, shirt
ise: rise, wise
ish: dish, swish
isk: disk, risk
iss: kiss, Swiss
ist: mist, wrist
it: hit, quit
itch: ditch, witch
ite: bite, write
ive: five, hive
ix: fix, six
o: do, to, who
o: go, no, so
oach: coach, poach
oad: road, toad
oak: soak, cloak
oal: coal, goal
oam: foam, roam
oan: Joan, loan
oar: boar, roar
oast: boast, coast
oat: boat, float
ob: job, throb
obe: robe, globe
ock: lock, stock
od: rod, sod
ode: code, rode
og: fog, clog
oil: boil, broil
oin: coin, join
oke: woke, spoke

een: seen, screen
eep: keep, sheep
old: gold, scold
ole: hole, stole
oll: droll, roll
ome: dome, home
one: cone, phone
ong: long, wrong
oo: too, zoo
ood: good, hood
ood: food, mood
ook: cook, took
ool: cool, fool
oom: room, bloom
oon: moon, spoon
oop: hoop, snoop
oot: boot, shoot
op: top, chop
ope: hope, slope
orch: porch, torch
ore: bore, snore
ork: cork, fork
om: horn, thorn
ort: fort, short
ose: rose, close
oss: boss, gloss
ost: cost, lost
ost: host, most
ot: got, trot
otch: notch, blotch
ote: note, quote
ough: rough, tough
ought: bought, brought
ould: could, would
ounce: bounce, pounce
ound: bound, found
ouse: house, mouse
out: pout, about
outh: mouth, south
ove: cove, grove

in: tin, spin
ince: since, prince
ove: dove, love
ow: how, chow
ow: slow, throw
owl: howl, growl
own: down, town
own: known, grown
ox: fox, pox
oy: boy, ploy
ub: cub, shrub
uck: duck, stuck
ud: mud, thud
ude: dude, rude
udge: fudge, judge
ue: sue, blue
uff: puff, stuff
ug: dug, plug
ule: rule, mule
ull: dull, gull
um: sum, chum
umb: numb, thumb
ump: bump, plump
un: run, spun
unch: bunch, hunch
une: June, tune
ung: hung, flung
unk: sunk, chunk
unt: bunt, hunt
ur: fur, blur
urn: burn, churn
urse: curse, nurse
us: bus, plus
ush: mush, crush
ust: dust, trust
ut: but, shut
ute: lute, flute
y: my, dry

VICKIE'S LEARNING CENTER DIRECTION CARDS

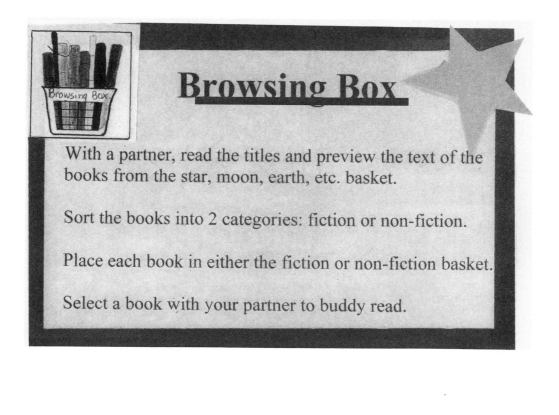

Buddy Reading

- Choose a different person in your group to read with.
- Sit beside your friend. Remember as one person reads aloud the other follows along in his/her book.
- Discuss each page as you read.
- Do your best reading with expression-try to sound like the characters and pay close attention to punctuation marks.

buddy reading

Browsing Box

Browsing Box

With a partner, read the titles and preview the text of the books from the star, moon, earth, etc. basket.

Sort the books into 2 categories: fiction or non-fiction.

Place each book in either the fiction or non-fiction basket.

Select a book with your partner to buddy read.

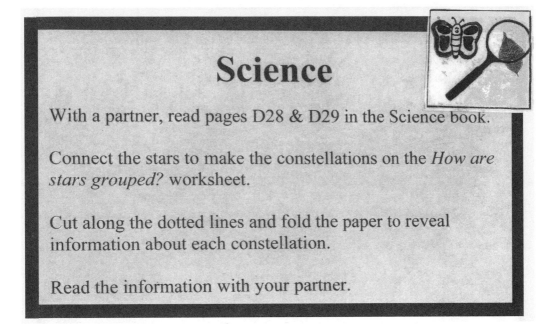

Science

With a partner, read pages D28 & D29 in the Science book.

Connect the stars to make the constellations on the *How are stars grouped?* worksheet.

Cut along the dotted lines and fold the paper to reveal information about each constellation.

Read the information with your partner.

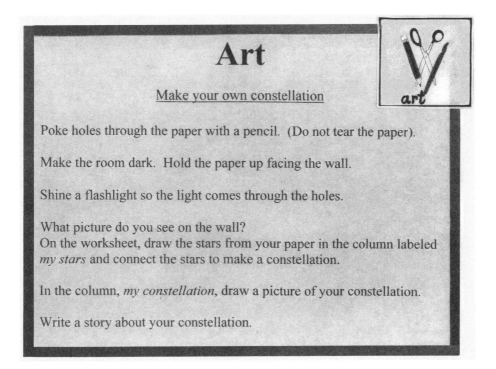

Art

Make your own constellation

Poke holes through the paper with a pencil. (Do not tear the paper).

Make the room dark. Hold the paper up facing the wall.

Shine a flashlight so the light comes through the holes.

What picture do you see on the wall?
On the worksheet, draw the stars from your paper in the column labeled *my stars* and connect the stars to make a constellation.

In the column, *my constellation*, draw a picture of your constellation.

Write a story about your constellation.

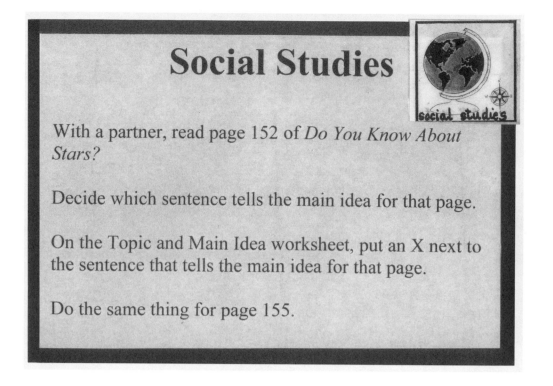

Social Studies

With a partner, read page 152 of *Do You Know About Stars?*

Decide which sentence tells the main idea for that page.

On the Topic and Main Idea worksheet, put an X next to the sentence that tells the main idea for that page.

Do the same thing for page 155.

REFERENCES

Adams, M. J. (1990). *Beginning to read.* Cambridge, MA: MIT Press.

Allen, J. (2002). *On the same page: Shared reading beyond the primary grades.* Portland, ME: Stenhouse.

Allington, R. L. (1983a). Fluency: The neglected reading goal. *The Reading Teacher, 36,* 556–561.

Allington, R. L. (1983b). The reading instruction provided readers of differing reading ability. *Elementary School Journal, 83,* 548–559.

Allington, R. L. (1991). The legacy of slow it down and make it more concrete. In J. Zutell & S. McCormick (Eds.), *Learner factors/teacher factors: Issues in literacy research and instruction* (pp. 19–30). Chicago: National Reading Conference.

Allington, R. L., & Nowak, R. (2004). "Proven programs" and other unscientific ideas. In D. Lapp, C. C. Block, E. J. Cooper, J. Flood, N. Roser, & J. V. Tinajero (Eds.), *Teaching all the children: Strategies for developing literacy in an urban setting* (pp. 93–102). New York: Guilford Press.

Alvarez, D., & Mehan, H. (2004). Providing educational opportunities for underrepresented students: The role of academic scaffolds and lesson study at the Preuss School, UCSD. In D. Lapp, C. C. Block, E. J. Cooper, J. Flood, N. Roser, & J. V. Tinajero (Eds.), *Teaching all the children: Strategies for developing literacy in an urban setting* (pp. 161–178). New York: Guilford Press.

Anderson, R. C. (1996). Research foundations to support wide reading. In V. Greaney (Ed.), *Promoting reading in developing countries* (pp. 55–77). Newark, DE: International Reading Association.

Anderson, R. C., & Nagy, W. E. (1992, Winter). The vocabulary conundrum. *American Educator,* pp. 14–18, 44–47.

Anderson, R. C., Wilson, P. T., & Fielding, L. G. (1988). Growth in reading and how children spend their time outside of school. *Reading Research Quarterly, 23,* 285–303.

Baker, K., & Allington, R. L. (2003). Strategies for literacy development for students with disabilities. In L. M. Morrow, L. B. Gambrell, & M. Pressley (Eds.),

Best practices in literacy instruction (2nd ed., pp. 287–306). New York: Guilford Press.

Barone, D. (2003/2004). Second grade is important: Literacy instruction and learning of young children in a high-poverty school. *Journal of Literacy Research, 35*(5), 965–1019.

Barr, R., & Dreeben, R. (1983). *How schools work.* Chicago: University of Chicago Press.

Barrera, R., & Jiménez, R. T. (2002). Bilingual teachers speak about the literacy instruction of bilingual Latino students. In B. M. Taylor & P. D. Pearson (Eds.), *Teaching reading: Effective schools, accomplished teachers* (pp. 325–360). Mahwah, NJ: Erlbaum.

Baumann, J. F., & Thomas, D. (1997). If you can pass Momma's tests, then she knows you're getting your education: A case study of support for literacy learning within an African-American family. *The Reading Teacher, 51,* 108–120.

Beck, I. L., McKeown, M. G., & Kucan, L. (2002). *Bringing words to life: Robust vocabulary instruction.* New York: Guilford Press.

Bernhardt, E. (1991). *Reading development in a second language.* Norwood, NJ: Ablex.

Blachowicz, C., & Fisher, P. J. (2002). *Teaching vocabulary in all classrooms* (2nd ed.). Upper Saddle River, NJ: Merrill/Prentice Hall.

Blachowicz, C., & Ogle, D. (2001). *Reading comprehension: Strategies for independent learners.* New York: Guilford Press.

Block, C. C. (1999). Comprehension: Crafting understanding. In L. B. Gambrell, L. M. Morrow, S. B. Neumann, & M. Pressley (Eds.), *Best practices in literacy instruction* (pp. 98–118). New York: Guilford Press.

Block, C. C., Oakar, M., & Hurt, N. (2002). The expertise of literacy teachers: A continuum from preschool to grade 5. *Reading Research Quarterly, 37*(2), 178–205.

Block, C. C., & Pressley, M. (2003). Best practices in comprehension instruction. In L. M. Morrow, L. B. Gambrell, & M. Pressley (Eds.), *Best practices in literacy instruction* (2nd ed., pp. 111–126). New York: Guilford Press.

Bond, G. L., & Dykstra, R. (1997). The cooperative research program in first-grade reading instruction. *Reading Research Quarterly, 32,* 348–427. (Original work published 1967)

Brisk, M., & Harrington, M. (2000). *Literacy and bilingualism: A handbook for all teachers.* Mahwah, NJ: Erlbaum.

Bromley, K. (1999). Key components of a sound writing program. In L. B. Gamrell, L. M. Morrow, S. B. Neuman, & M. Pressley (Eds.), *Best practices in literacy instruction* (pp. 152–1740. New York: Guilford Press.

Bromley, K. (2003). Building a sound writing program. In L. M. Morrow, L. B. Gambrell, & M. Pressley (Eds.), *Best practices in literacy instruction* (2nd ed., pp. 143–166). New York: Guilford Press.

Caldwell, J. S. (2002). *Reading assessment: A primer for teachers and tutors.* New York: Guilford Press.

Calkins, L. M. (1994). *The art of teaching writing.* Portsmouth, NH: Heinemann.

Carlo, M. S., August, D., McLaughlin, B., Snow, C. E., Dressler, C., Lippman, D. N., Lively, T. J., & White, C. E. (2004). Closing the gap: Addressing the vocabulary needs of English-language learners in bilingual and mainstream classrooms. *Reading Research Quarterly, 39*(2), 188–215.

Clark, M. (1976). *Young fluent readers: What they can teach us.* London: Heinemann.

Clay, M. (1979). *The early detection of reading difficulties: A diagnostic survey with recovery procedures.* Portsmouth, NH: Heinemann.

Clay, M. M. (2000). *Running records for classroom teachers.* Portsmouth, NH: Heinemann.

Cohen, P. A., Kulik, J. A., & Kulik, C. L. C. (1982). Educational outcomes of tutoring: A meta-analysis of findings. *American Educational Research Journal, 19,* 237–248.

Cooper, J. D., & Kiger, N. D. (2005). *Literacy assessment: Helping teachers plan instruction* (2nd ed.). Boston: Houghton Mifflin.

Corno, L. (1989). What it means to be literate about classrooms. In D. Bloome (Ed.), *Classrooms and literacy* (pp. 29–52). Norwood, NJ: Ablex.

Cunningham, A., & Stanovich, K. (1997). Early reading acquisition and its relation to reading experience and ability 10 years later. *Developmental Psychology, 33,* 934–945.

Cunningham, P. M. (2003). What research says about teaching phonics. In L. M. Morrow, L. B. Gambrell, & M. Pressley (Eds.), *Best practices in literacy instruction* (2nd ed., pp. 65–86). New York: Guilford Press.

Cunningham, P. M. (2005). *Phonics they use: Words for reading and writing* (4th ed.). Boston: Allyn & Bacon.

Cunningham, P. M., Hall, D. P., & Defee, M. (1991). Non-ability grouped, multilevel instruction: A year in a first-grade classroom. *The Reading Teacher, 44,* 566–571.

Delgado-Gaitan, C. (1992). School matters in the Mexican-American home: Socializing children to education. *American Educational Research Journal, 29*(3), 495–513.

Delgado-Gaitan, C., & Trueba, H. (1991). *Crossing cultural borders: Education for immigrant families in America.* New York: Falmer Press.

Duke, N. K. (2000a). 3.6 minutes per day: The scarcity of informational texts in first grade. *Reading Research Quarterly, 35*(2), 202–224.

Duke, N. K. (2000b). For the richer it's richer: Print environments and experiences offered to first-grade students in very low- and very high-SES school districts. *American Educational Research Journal, 37,* 441–478.

Durkin, D. (1966). *Children who read early.* New York: Teachers College Press.

Edwards, P. A., Pleasants, H. M., & Franklin, S. H. (1999). *A path to follow: Learning to listen to parents.* Portsmouth, NH: Heinemann.

Elley, W. B. (1996). Using book floods to raise literacy levels in developing countries. In V. Greaney (Ed.), *Promoting reading in developing countries* (pp. 148–162). Newark, DE: International Reading Association.

Englert, C. S., & Dunsmore, K. L. (2002). Scientific literacy and diverse learners:

Supporting the acquisition of disciplinary ways of knowing in inclusion class-rooms. In B. M. Taylor & P. D. Pearson (Eds.), *Teaching reading: Effective schools, accomplished teachers* (pp. 309–334). Mahwah, NJ: Erlbaum.

Epstein, J. (1986). Parents' reactions to teacher practices of parent involvement. *Elementary School Journal, 86,* 277–294.

Epstein, J. L. (2001). *School, family, and community partnerships.* Boulder, CO: Westview Press.

Farkas, S., Johnson, J., & Duffett, A. (2003). *Stand by me: What teachers really think about unions, merit pay, and other professional matters* New York: Public Agenda. Available at www.edexcellence.net.

Fielding, L., & Roller, C. (1992). Making difficult books accessible and easy books acceptable. *The Reading Teacher, 45,* 678–685.

Fisher, D., Flood, J., & Lapp, D. (2003). Material matters: Using children's litera-ture to charm readers (or why Harry Potter and the Princess Diaries matter). In L. M. Morrow, L. B. Gambrell, & M. Pressley (Eds.), *Best practices in literacy instruction* (2nd ed., pp. 167–186). New York: Guilford Press.

Fitzgerald, J. (1995). English as a second language learners; cognitive reading pro-cesses: A review of research in the United States. *Review of Educational Research, 65,* 145–190.

Fitzgerald, J., & Nobbit, G. W. (1999). About hopes, aspirations, and uncertainty: First-grade English-language learners' emergent literacy. *Journal of Literacy Research, 65,* 133–182.

Ford, M. P., & Opitz, M. F. (2002). Using centers to engage children during guided reading time: Intensifying learning experiences away from the teacher. *The Reading Teacher, 56,* 710–717.

Fountas, I. C., & Pinnell, G. S. (1996). *Guided reading: Good first teaching for chil-dren.* Portsmouth, NH: Heinemann.

Fountas, I. C., & Pinnell, G. S. (2002). *Phonics lessons: Letters, words, and how they work.* Westport, CT: Greenwood.

Fractor, J. S., Woodruff, M. C., Martinez, M., & Teale, W. H. (1993). Let's not miss an opportunity to promote voluntary reading: Classroom libraries in the ele-mentary school. *The Reading Teacher, 46,* 476–484.

Freebody, P., & Anderson, R. C. (1983). Effects of vocabulary difficulty, text cohe-sion, and schema availability on reading comprehension. *Reading Research Quarterly, 18,* 277–294.

Galda, L., & Cullinan, B. E. (2000). Reading aloud from culturally diverse litera-ture. In D. S. Strickland & L. M. Morrow (Eds.), *Beginning reading and writing* (pp. 134–142). New York: Teachers College Press.

Gambrell, L. B. (1996). Creating classroom cultures that foster reading motivation. *The Reading Teacher, 50,* 14–25.

Gambrell, L. B. (2004). Literacy motivation: Implications for urban classrooms. In D. Lapp, C. C. Block, E. J. Cooper, J. Flood, N. Roser, & J. V. Tinajero (Eds.), *Teaching all the children: Strategies for developing literacy in an urban setting* (pp. 193–201). New York: Guilford Press.

Gambrell, L. B., & Dromskey, A. (2000). Fostering reading comprehension. In D.

S. Strickland & L. M. Morrow (Eds.), *Beginning reading and writing* (pp. 143–153). New York: Teachers College Press.

Garcia, G. E. (1991). Factors influencing the English reading test performance of Spanish-speaking Hispanic students. *Reading Research Quarterly, 26*, 371–392.

Gillespie, J. T. (2001). *Best books for children: Pre-school through grade 6* (6th ed.). Westport, CT: Libraries Unlimited.

Goatley, V. J., Brock, C. H., & Raphael, T. E. (1995). Diverse learners participating in regular education book clubs. *Reading Research Quarterly, 30*, 352–380.

Good, T. L., & Marshall, S. (1984). Do students learn more in heterogeneous or homogeneous groups? In P. L. Peterson, L. C. Wilkinson, & M. Hallinan (Eds.), *The social context of instruction: Group organization and group processes* (pp. 15–38). New York: Academic Press.

Goodman, K. (1965). A linguistic study of cues and miscues in reading. *Elementary English, 42*, 639–643.

Goodman, Y. (1982). Kidwatching: Evaluating written language development. *Australian Journal of Reading, 5*, 120–128.

Graves, D. (1994). *A fresh look at writing*. Portsmouth, NH: Heinemann.

Graves, M. F., Juel, C., & Graves, B. B. (2003). *Teaching reading in the 21st century* (3rd ed.). Boston: Allyn & Bacon.

Graves, M. F., & Watts-Taffe, S. (2002). The place of word consciousness in a research-based reading program. In A. E. Farstrup & S. J. Samuels (Eds.), *What research has to say about reading instruction* (pp. 140–165). Newark, DE: International Reading Association.

Gredler, M. E., & Johnson, R. L. (2004). *Assessment in the literacy classroom*. Boston: Pearson.

Guthrie, J. R., Alvermann, D. E., & Au, K. H. (1998). *Engaging reading: Processes, practices, and policy implications*. New York: Teachers College Press.

Guthrie, J. R., & Wigfield, A. (1999). *How motivation fits into a science of reading*. Mahwah, NJ: Erlbaum.

Guthrie, J. T., & Wigfield, A. (2000). Engagement and motivation in reading. In M. L. Kamil, P. B. Mosenthal, P. D. Pearson, & R. Barr (Eds.), *Engagement and motivation in reading* (Vol. 3, pp. 403–422). Mahwah, NJ: Erlbaum.

Hall, D. P., & Cunningham, P. M. (1996). Becoming literate in first and second grades: Six years of multimethod, multilevel instruction. In D. J. Leu, C. K. Kinzer, & K. H. Hinchman (Eds.), *Literacies for the 21st century: Research and practice* (pp. 295–304). Chicago: National Reading Conference.

Harp, B., & Brewer, J. A. (2000). Assessing reading and writing in the early years. In D. S. Strickland & L. M. Morrow (Eds.), *Beginning reading and writing* (pp. 154–167). New York: Teachers College Press.

Heath, S. B. (1983). *Ways with words*. Cambridge, UK: Cambridge University Press.

Hefflin, B. R., & Hartman, D. K. (2002). Using writing to improve comprehension: A review of writing-to-reading research. In C. C. Block, L. B. Gambrell, & M. Pressley (Eds.), *Improving comprehension instruction: Rethinking research, theory, and classroom practice* (pp. 199–229). San Francisco: Jossey-Bass.

Henderson, A. T., & Berla, N. (Eds.). (1994). *A new generation of evidence: The fam-*

ily is critical to student achievement. Washington, DC: Center for Law and Education.

Hiebert, E. H. (1983). An examination of ability grouping for reading instruction. *Reading Research Quarterly, 18*, 231–255.

Hiebert, E. H. (1994). A small-group literacy intervention with Chapter 1 students. In E. H. Hiebert & B. M. Taylor (Eds.), *Getting reading right from the start: Effective early literacy interventions* (pp. 107–122). Needham, MA: Allyn & Bacon.

Holdaway, D. (1979). *The foundations of literacy.* Sydney, Australia: Ashton Scholastic.

Huck, C. S., Hepler, S., Hickman, J., & Kiefer, B. Z. (2001). *Children's literature in the elementary school* (7th ed.). Boston: McGraw-Hill.

International Reading Association. (2000). *Making a difference means making it different: Honoring children's rights to excellent reading instruction.* Newark, DE: International Reading Association.

International Reading Association and National Council of Teachers of English. (1996). *Standards for the English Language Arts.* Newark, DE: International Reading Association.

Jackson, J. B., Paratore, J. R., Chard, D. J., & Garnick, S. (1999). An early intervention supporting the literacy learning of children experiencing substantial difficulty. *Learning Disabilities Research and Practice, 14*, 254–268.

Jenkins, J. R., Jewell, M., Leicester, N., O'Connor, R., Jenkins, L. M., & Troutner, N. M. (1994). Accommodations for individual differences without classroom ability groups: An experiment in restructuring. *Exceptional Children, 60*, 344–348.

Johnson, D. W., Maruyama, G., Johnson, R., & Nelson, D. (1981). Effects of cooperative, competitive, and individualistic goal structures: A meta-analysis. *Psychological Bulletin, 89*, 47–62.

Johnson, D., & Pearson, P. D. (1984). *Teaching reading vocabulary.* New York: Holt, Rinehart & Winston.

Johnston, P. H. (1997). *Knowing literacy: Constructive literacy assessment.* York, ME: Stenhouse.

Johnston, P. H., & Clay, M. M. (1997). Recording oral reading. In P. H. Johnston, *Knowing literacy: Constructive literacy assessment* (pp. 192–211). York, ME: Stenhouse.

Jordan, G. E., Snow, C. E., & Porche, M. V. (2000). Project EASE: The effect of a family literacy project on kindergarten students' early literacy skills. *Reading Research Quarterly, 35*, 524–546.

Juel, C. (1988). Learning to read and write: A longitudinal study of fifty-four children from first through fourth grade. *Journal of Educational Psychology, 80*, 437–447.

Juel, C. (1990). Effects of reading group assignment on reading development in first and second grade. *Journal of Reading Behavior, 22*, 233–254.

Juel, C., & Deffes, R. (2004). Making words stick. *Educational Leadership, 61*, 31–34.

Juel, C., & Roper-Schneider, D. (1985). The influence of basal readers on first grade reading. *Reading Research Quarterly, 20*, 134–151.

Knapp, M. S. (1995). *Teaching for meaning in high-poverty classrooms*. New York: Teachers College Press.

Koskinen, P. S., & Blum, I. H. (1986). Paired repeated reading: A classroom strategy for developing fluent reading. *The Reading Teacher, 40*, 70–75.

Kriete, R., & Betchel, L. (2002). *The morning meeting book*. Greenfield, MA: Northeast Foundation for Children.

Krol-Sinclair, B. (1996). Connecting home and school literacies: Immigrant parents with limited formal education as classroom storybook readers. In D. J. Leu, C. K. Kinzer, & K. A. Hinchman (Eds.), *Literacies for the 21st century: Research and practice* (pp. 270–283). Chicago: National Reading Conference.

Kuhn, M. R. (2003). Fluency in the classroom: Strategies for whole-class and group work. In L. M. Morrow, L. B. Gambrell, & M. Pressley (Eds.), *Best practices in literacy instruction* (2nd ed., pp. 127–142). New York: Guilford Press.

LaBerge, D., & Samuels, S. J. (1974). Toward a theory of automatic information processing in reading. *Cognitive Psychology, 6*, 293–323.

Lapp, D., Fisher, D., Flood, J., & Goss-Moore, K. (2002). Selecting materials for the literacy program. In S. B. Wepner, D. S. Strickland, & J. T. Feeley (Eds.), *The administration and supervision of reading programs* (pp. 83–94). New York: Teachers College Press.

Lapp, D., Flood, J., & Roser, N. (2000). Still standing: Timeless strategies for teaching the language arts. In D. S. Strickland & L. M. Morrow (Eds.), *Beginning reading and writing* (pp. 183–194). New York: Teachers College Press.

Lareau, A. (1989). *Home advantage: Social class and parental intervention*. New York: Falmer Press.

Lazar, A. M. (2004). *Learning to be literacy teachers in urban schools: Stories of growth and change*. Newark, DE: International Reading Association.

Lima, C., & Lima, J. (2001). *A to zoo: Subject access to children's picture books* (6th ed.). New Providence, NJ: Libraries Unlimited.

Lou, Y., Abrami, P. C., Spence, C., Poulsen, C., Chambers, B., & d'Apollonia, S. (1996). Within-class grouping: A meta-analysis. *Review of Educational Research, 66*, 423–458.

Mandler, J. M., & Johnson, N. S. (1977). Remembrance of things parsed: Story structure and recall. *Cognitive Psychology, 9*, 111–151.

Martinez, M., Roser, N. L., & Strecker, S. (1998/1999). "I never thought I could be a star": A Readers' Theatre ticket to fluency. *The Reading Teacher, 52*, 326–334.

McCormack, R. L. (1997). Eavesdropping on second graders' peer talk about African trickster tales. In J. R. Paratore & R. L. McCormack (Eds.), *Peer talk in the classroom: Learning from research* (pp. 26–44). Newark, DE: International Reading Association.

McCracken, R. A., & McCracken, M. J. (1978). Modeling is the key to sustained silent reading. *The Reading Teacher, 31*, 406–408.

McKenna, M. C., & Stahl, S. A. (2003). *Assessment for reading instruction*. New York: Guilford Press.

Mehan, H., Villanueva, I., Hubbard, L., & Lintz, A. (1996). *Constructing school success: The consequences of untracking low-achieving students.* New York: Cambridge University Press.

Morrow, L. M. (1989). *Literacy development in the early years.* Angle Cliffs, NJ: Prentice Hall.

Morrow, L. M. (2000). Organizing and managing a language arts block. In D. S. Strickland & L. M. Morrow (Eds.), *Beginning reading and writing* (pp. 83–98). New York: Teachers College Press.

Morrow, L. M. (2002). *The literacy center: Contexts for reading and writing* (2nd ed.). Portland, ME: Stenhouse.

Morrow, L. M., & Asbury, E. (2003). Current practices in early literacy development. In L. M. Morrow, L. B. Gambrell, & M. Pressley (Eds.), *Best practices in literacy instruction* (2nd ed., pp. 43–64). New York: Guilford Press.

Morrow, L. M., & Gambrell, L. B. (2000). Literature-based reading instruction. In M. L. Kamil, P. B. Mosenthal, P. D. Pearson, & R. Barr (Eds.), *Handbook of reading research* (Vol. 3, pp. 563–586). Mahwah, NJ: Erlbaum.

Nagy, W. E. (1986). *Teaching vocabulary to improve reading comprehension.* Newark, DE: International Reading Association.

Nagy, W. E. (1997). On the role of context in first- and second-language vocabulary learning. In N. Schmitt & M. McCarthy (Eds.), *Vocabulary: Description, acquisition and pedagogy* (pp. 64–83). Cambridge, UK: Cambridge University Press.

National Clearinghouse for Comprehensive School Reform. (2001). Taking stock: Lessons on comprehensive school reform from policy, practice, and research. *Benchmarks, 2,* 1–11.

National Reading Panel Report. (2000). *Teaching children to read: An evidence-based assessment of the scientific research literature on reading and its implications for reading instruction: Reports of the subgroups.* Washington, DC: National Institute of Child Health and Human Development.

New Standards Primary Literacy Committee. (1999). *Reading and writing grade by grade: Primary literacy standards for kindergarten through third grade.* Pittsburgh, PA: National Center on Education and the Economy and University of Pittsburgh.

Ogle, D. M. (1986). K-W-L: A teaching model that develops active reading of expository text. *The Reading Teacher, 39,* 564–570.

O'Shea, L. J., Sindelar, P. T., & O'Shea, D. J. (1985). The effects of repeated readings and attentional cues on reading fluency and comprehension. *Journal of Reading Behavior, 17,* 129–142.

Paratore, J. R. (2000). Grouping for instruction in literacy: What we've learned about what's working and what's not. *The California Reader, 33*(4), 2–10.

Paratore, J. R. (2001). *Opening doors, opening opportunities: Family literacy in an urban community.* Needham Heights, MA: Allyn & Bacon.

Paratore, J. R. (2002). Home and school together: Helping beginning readers succeed. In A. E. Farstrup & S. J. Samuels (Eds.), *What research has to say about reading instruction* (pp. 48–68). Newark, DE: International Reading Association.

Paratore, J. R., Fountas, I. C, Jenkins, C. A., Matthews, M. E., Ouellette, J. M., & Sheehan, N. M. (1992). *Classroom assessment in literacy: Using what we know to construct literacy portfolios.* Position paper published by the Massachusetts Reading Association, West Barnstable, MA.

Paratore, J. R., Garnick, S., & Lewis, T. (1997). Watching teachers watch children talk about books. In J. R. Paratore & R. L. McCormack (Eds.), *Peer talk in the classroom: Learning from research* (pp. 207–232). Newark, DE: International Reading Association.

Paratore, J. R., Hindin, A., Krol-Sinclair, B., & Durán, P. (1999). Discourse between teachers and Latino parents during conferences based on home literacy portfolios. *Education and Urban Society, 32,* 58–82.

Paratore, J. R., Homza, A., Krol-Sinclair, B., Lewis-Barrow, T., Melzi, G., Stergis, R., & Haynes, H. (1995). Shifting boundaries in home and school responsibilities: Involving immigrant parents in the construction of literacy portfolios. *Research in the Teaching of English, 29,* 367–389.

Paratore, J. R., & Indrisano, R. (1987). Intervention assessment in reading comprehension. *The Reading Teacher, 40,* 778–783.

Paratore, J. R., Melzi, G., & Krol-Sinclair, B. (1999). *What should we expect of family literacy? Experiences of Latino children whose parents participate in an intergenerational literacy program.* Newark, DE: International Reading Association.

Paratore, J. R., Melzi, G., & Krol-Sinclair, B. (2003). Learning about the literate lives of Latino parents. In D. M. Barone & L. M. Morrow (Eds.), *Research-based practice in early literacy* (pp. 101–120). New York: Guilford Press.

Pearson, P. D., & Gallagher, M. C. (1983). The instruction of reading comprehension. *Contemporary Educational Psychology, 8,* 3317–3344.

Pearson, P. D., & Johnson, D. (1984). *Teaching reading comprehension.* New York: Holt, Rinehart & Winston.

Piazza, C. (2002). *Journeys: The teaching of writing in the elementary classroom.* Englewood Cliffs, NJ: Prentice Hall.

Pinnell, G. S., & Fountas, I. C. (1998). *Word matters: Teaching phonics and spelling in reading/writing classrooms.* Portsmouth, NH: Heinemann.

Pressley, M., Allington, R. L., Wharton-McDonald, R., Block, C. C., & Morrow, L. M. (2001). *Learning to read: Lessons from exemplary first-grade classrooms.* New York: Guilford Press.

Pressley, M., Ed-Dinary, P. B., Gaskins, I., Schuder, T., Gergman, J., Almasi, J., & Brown, R. (1992). Beyond direct explanation: Transactional instruction of reading comprehension strategies. *Elementary School Journal, 92,* 511–554.

Raphael, T. E., & Brock, C. H. (1993). Mei: Learning the literacy culture in an urban elementary school. In D. J. Leu & C. K. Kinzer (Eds.), *Examining central issues in literacy research, theory, and practice* (pp. 179–188). Chicago: National Reading Conference.

Raphael, T. E., & McMahon, S. I. (1997). *The Book Club connection: Literacy, language, and classroom talk.* New York: Teachers College Press.

Raphael, T. E., Brock, C. H., & Wallace, S. M. as(1996). Encouraging quality peer talk with diverse students in mainstream classrooms: Learning from and with teachers. In J. R. Paratore & R. L. McCormack (Eds.), *Peer talk in the classroom: Learning from research* (pp. 176–206). Newark, DE: International Reading Association.

Rasinski, T. V. (1990). Effects of repeated reading and listening-while-reading on reading fluency. *Journal of Educational Research, 83,* 147–150.

Rasinski, T. V., & Padak, N. D. (2001). *From phonics to fluency: Effective teaching of decoding and reading fluency in the elementary school.* New York: Longman.

Rhodes, L. K., & Shanklin, N. L. (1993). *Windows into literacy.* Portsmouth, NH: Heinemann.

Rosenshine, B., & Stevens, R. (1984). Classroom instruction in reading. In P. D. Pearson, R. Barr, M. L. Kamil, & P. Mosenthal (Eds.), *Handbook of reading research* (Vol. 1, pp. 745–798). New York: Longman.

Roser, N. L., May, L. A., Martinez, M., Keehn, S., Harmon, J. M., & O'Neal, S. (2003). Stepping into character(s): Using Readers' Theatre with bilingual fourth graders. In R. L. McCormack & J. R. Paratore (Eds.), *After early intervention, then what? Teaching struggling readers in grades 3 and beyond* (pp. 40–69). Newark, DE: International Reading Association.

Samuels, S. J. (1979). The method of repeated readings. *The Reading Teacher, 32,* 403–408.

Scott, J. A. (2004). Scaffolding vocabulary learning: Ideas for equity in urban settings. In D. Lapp, C. C. Block, E. J. Cooper, J. Flood, N. Roser, & J. V. Tinajero (Eds.), *Teaching all the children: Strategies for developing literacy in an urban setting* (pp. 275–293). New York: Guilford Press.

Senechal, M., & Cornell, E. H. (1993). Vocabulary acquisition through shared reading experiences. *Reading Research Quarterly, 28*(4), 360–374.

Sharan, S. (1980). Cooperative learning in small groups: Recent methods and effects on achievement, attitudes, and ethnic relations. *Review of Educational Research, 50,* 241–271.

Shockley, B., Michalove, B., & Allen, J. (1995). *Engaging families: Connecting home and school literacy communities.* Portsmouth, NH: Heinemann.

Short, K. G., & Klassen, C. (1993). Literature circles: Hearing children's voices. In B. Cullinan (Ed.), *Children's voices: Talk in the classroom* (pp. 377–385). Newark, DE: International Reading Association.

Short, K., & Pierce, K. M. (Eds.). (1998). *Talking about books: Literacy discussion groups in K–8 classrooms.* Portsmouth, NH: Heinemann.

Slavin, R. E. (1980). Cooperative learning. *Review of Educational Research, 50,* 315–342.

Slavin, R. E. (1987). *Ability grouping and student achievement in elementary school: A best evidence synthesis.* Baltimore, MD: Center for Research on Elementary and Secondary Schools, Johns Hopkins University.

Snow, C. E., Burns, S. M., & Griffin, P. (1998). *Preventing reading difficulties in young children.* Washington, DC: National Academy Press.

Snow, C. E., & Sweet, A. P. (2002). Reading for comprehension. In A. P. Sweet & C. E. Snow (Eds.), *Rethinking reading comprehension* (pp. 1–12). New York: Guilford Press.

Stanovich, K. E. (1986). Matthew effects in reading: Some consequences of individual differences in the acquisition of literacy. *Reading Research Quarterly, 21,* 360–407.

Stanovich, K. E. (2000). *Progress in understanding reading: Scientific foundations and new frontiers.* New York: Guilford Press.

Stein, N. L., & Glenn, C. (1979). An analysis of story comprehension. In R. Freedle (Ed.), *Advances in Discourse Processing: Vol. 2. New directions in discourse processing* (pp. 53–120). Norwood, NJ: Ablex.

Stevens, R. J., Madden, N. A., Slavin, R. E., & Famish, A. M. (1987). Cooperative integrated reading and composition: Two field experiments. *Reading Research Quarterly, 22,* 433–454.

Stevens, R. J., & Slavin, E., (1995). Effects of a cooperative learning approach to reading and writing on academically handicapped and nonhandicapped students. *Elementary School Journal, 95,* 241–262.

Street, B. (1995). *Social literacies: Critical approaches to literacy in development, ethnography, and education.* New York: Longman.

Swap, S. M. (1993). *Developing home–school partnerships: From concepts to practice.* New York: Teachers College Press.

Taylor, B. M., & Pearson, P. D. (2002). *Teaching reading: Effective schools, accomplished teachers.* Mahwah, NJ: Erlbaum.

Taylor, B. M., Strait, J., & Medo, M. A. (1994). Early intervention in reading: Supplemental instruction for groups of low-achieving children provided by first-grade teachers. In E. H. Hiebert & B. M. Taylor (Eds.), *Getting reading right from the start: Effective early literacy interventions* (pp. 107–122). Needham, MA: Allyn & Bacon.

Taylor, D., & Dorsey-Gaines, C. (1988). *Growing up literate: Learning from inner-city families.* Portsmouth, NH: Heinemann.

Teale, W. H. (1986). Home background and young children's literacy development. In W. H. Teale & E. Sulzby (Eds.), *Emergent literacy: Writing and reading* (pp. 173–206). Norwood, NJ: Ablex.

Teale, W. H., & Yokota, J. (2000). Beginning reading and writing: perspectives on instruction. In D. S. Strickland & L. M. Morrow (Eds.), *Beginning reading and writing* (pp. 3–21). New York: Teachers College Press.

Temple, C., Martinez, M., Yokota, J., & Naylor, A. (2002). *Children's books in children's hands: An introduction to their literature* (2nd ed.). Boston: Allyn & Bacon.

Turpie, J. J., & Paratore, J. R. (1995). Using repeated reading to promote success in a heterogeneously grouped first grade. In C. Kinzer, K. A. Hinchman, & D. L. Leu (Eds.), *Perspectives on literacy research and practice* (pp. 255–263). Chicago: National Reading Conference.

Valdés, G. (1996). *Con respeto: Bridging the differences between culturally diverse families and schools.* New York: Teachers College Press.

Vasquez, O., Pease-Alvarez, L., & Shannon, S. M. (1994). *Pushing boundaries: Language and culture in a Mexicano community.* New York: Cambridge University Press.

Verhoeven, L. T. (1990). Acquisition of reading in a second language. *Reading Research Quarterly, 25,* 90–114.

Vygotsky, L. S. (1978). *Mind in society: The development of higher psychological processes.* Cambridge, MA: Harvard University Press.

Winograd, P., Flores-Dueñas, L., & Arrington, H. (2003). Best practices in assessment. In L. M. Morrow, L. B. Gambrell, & M. Pressley (Eds.), *Best practices in literacy instruction* (2nd ed., pp. 201–240). New York: Guilford Press.

Worthy, J., & McCool, S. (1996). Students that say they hate to read: The importance of opportunity, choice, and access. In D. J. Leu, G. K. Keizer, & K. A. Hinchman (Eds.), *Literacies for the 21st century: Research and Practice, 45th yearbook of the National Reading Conference* (pp. 245–256). Chicago: National Reading Conference.

Worthy, J., & Roser, N. (2004). Flood ensurance: When children have books they can and want to read. In D. Lapp, C. C. Block, E. J. Cooper, J. Flood, N. Roser, & J. V. Tinajero (Eds.), *Teaching all the children to read: Strategies for developing literacy in an urban setting* (pp. 179–192). New York: Guilford Press.

Yopp, H. K. (1992). Developing phonemic awareness in young children. *The Reading Teacher, 45,* 696–703.

Yopp, H. K. (1995). Yopp–Singer Test of Phoneme Segmentation. *The Reading Teacher, 49,* 40–49.

Ziegler, R. J. (1993). How to help kids enjoy reading. *Principal, 72,* 44–48.

CHILDREN'S BOOKS

Allard, H. (1982). *Miss Nelson is missing!* Boston: Houghton Mifflin.

Baylor, B. (1976). *Hawk, I'm your brother.* New York: Macmillan.

Bloksberg, R. (1995). *The hole in Harry's pocket.* New York: Hyperion Books for Children.

Colfer, E. (2003). *Artemis Fowl.* New York: Hyperion Books for Children.

Cooney, B. (1985). *Miss Rumphius.* Madison, WI: Turtleback Books.

Dayrell, E. (1990). *Why the sun and moon live in the sky.* Boston: Houghton Mifflin.

Eager, E. (1999). *Seven day magic.* New York: Harcourt Children's Books.

Fox, M. (1992). *Night noises.* New York: Trumpet Books.

Gibbons, G. (1999). *Stargazers.* New York: Holiday House.

Ibbotson, E. (1998). *Secret of platform 13.* New York: Penguin Group.

LaFontaine. (1989). *The fox and the stork.* Boston: Houghton Mifflin.

Lasky, K. (2002). *The emperor's old clothes.* New York: Voyager Books.

Nimmo, J. (2003). *Midnight for Charlie Bone.* New York: Scholastic.

Rey, H. A. (1976). *The stars: A new way to see them.* Boston: Houghton Mifflin.

Rowling, J. K. (2000). *Harry Potter and the goblet of fire.* New York: Scholastic.

Scott-Foresman. (1994). *Discover the wonder: Earth and Sky.* Boston: Pearson Group.

Stefoff, R. (1996). *Chameleon.* New York: Benchmark Books.

Stefoff, R. (1997). *Jellyfish.* New York: Benchmark Books.

Stefoff, R. (1998). *Ant.* New York: Benchmark Books.

Stefoff, R. (1998). *Crab.* New York: Benchmark Books.

INDEX

Page numbers followed by *f* indicate figure.